The Kuyper Center Review

New Essays in Reformed Theology and Public Life

The Kuyper Center Review publishes substantial essays of a historical or critical kind that relate the tradition of Reformed theology to issues of public life. Although it will take a special interest in the writings of Abraham Kuyper (1837-1920) and in the neo-Calvinist style of thought that he initiated, the aim is also to provide a vehicle for the widest-ranging exploration of the history and contemporary relevance of Reformed theology to important topics in politics, economics, and culture. Contributions from a variety of disciplines—history, philosophy, the humanities, and social sciences, as well as theology—are warmly welcomed.

The Kuyper Center Review

VOLUME 1 *Politics, Religion, and Sphere Sovereignty*

Edited by

Gordon Graham

WILLIAM B. EERDMANS PUBLISHING COMPANY

GRAND RAPIDS, MICHIGAN / CAMBRIDGE, U.K.

© 2010 Princeton Theological Seminary

Published 2010 by
Wm. B. Eerdmans Publishing Co.
2140 Oak Industrial Drive N.E., Grand Rapids, Michigan 49505 /
P.O. Box 163, Cambridge CB3 9PU U.K.

Printed in the United States of America

16 15 14 13 12 11 10   7 6 5 4 3 2 1

Library of Congress Cataloging-in-Publication Data

The Kuyper Center review / edited by Gordon Graham.
         p.   cm.
    Includes bibliographical references.
    ISBN 978-0-8028-6491-8 (v. 1: pbk.: alk. paper)
    1. Christianity and politics — Congresses. 2. Kuyper, Abraham, 1837-1920 —
    Congresses.   I. Graham, Gordon, 1949 July 15-

    BR115.P7K89   2010
    261.7 — dc22

                                                        2009043721

www.eerdmans.com

Contents

Contents

Editorial

This volume of essays is one of a number of initiatives on the part of the Abraham Kuyper Center for Public Theology at Princeton Theological Seminary to stimulate new work in the broad area of Reformed theology and public life. The Center was established in both admiration and emulation for the work of Abraham Kuyper, whose life as pastor, theologian, journalist, and politician provides such a remarkable example of how confidence in the truth of a Christian conception of the world can be expressed in both theory and practice. Since its establishment, experience has shown that there is widespread and serious interest, not just in Kuyper but also in Kuyperian themes, among a new generation of thinkers. The aim of the *Kuyper Center Review* is to provide a forum in which work by this new generation can be found alongside that of acknowledged experts.

Our hope is that this is an inaugural volume, to be followed by an annual publication for many years to come. Its contents derive in large part from revised versions of a small selection of the papers delivered at the 2008 Kuyper Conference in Princeton. The theme of that conference was "Sphere Sovereignty and Civil Society," with the result that most of the papers published here have a broadly "political" character, some addressing contemporary issues, some of a more historical nature. Of special interest in this issue (and not arising from the conference) is a summary/translation of Kuyper's 1907 essay "The Enigma of Islam," an essay that has never been published in English.

In future volumes we also hope to publish work that has been stimulated by our annual April conference. But the *Review* will not be tied to the conference theme. Our editorial policy is to welcome the submission of papers at any time, and on any subject that falls within the remit of the Center. With the exception of special lectures delivered by invitation — such as the Kuyper Prize Lecture — all submissions will be subject to peer review, thereby ensuring that the work we publish is not only new, but also of the highest standard.

Contributors

JOHN R. BOWLIN is the Rimmer and Ruth de Vries Associate Professor of Reformed Theology and Public Life at Princeton Theological Seminary. He is the author of *Contingency and Fortune in Aquinas's Ethics* (Cambridge University Press, 1999) and numerous articles. He has recently completed a book on tolerance and forbearance.

JAMES D. BRATT is Professor of History at Calvin College. He is the editor of *Abraham Kuyper: A Centennial Anthology* (Eerdmans, 1998) and author of *Dutch Calvinism in Modern America: A History of a Conservative Subculture* (Eerdmans, 1984).

JONATHAN CHAPLIN is the first Director of the Kirby Laing Institute for Christian Ethics in Cambridge, U.K., a position he took up in September 2006. From 1999 to 2006 he served as Associate Professor of Political Theory at the Institute for Christian Studies (ICS) in Toronto, Canada, holding the Dooyeweerd Chair in Social and Political Philosophy from 2004 to 2006.

MICHAEL J. DEMOOR was a graduate student at the Institute for Christian Studies in Toronto and is now Assistant Professor of Social Philosophy in Politics, History and Economics at The King's University College in Edmonton, Alberta.

JAMES J. S. FOSTER is a Ph.D. candidate at Princeton Theological Seminary and winner of the 2008 Kuyper Research Fellowship. His research relates to the philosophy of Thomas Reid, on whom he has published in the *Journal of Scottish Philosophy.*

GORDON GRAHAM is Henry Luce III Professor of Philosophy and the Arts at Princeton Theological Seminary. He is the author of numerous papers and several books, including most recently *The Re-enchantment of the World: Art versus Religion* (Oxford University Press, 2007), which is based on the Stanton Lectures in Philosophy of Religion delivered at the University of Cambridge.

GEORGE HARINCK is Professor of the History of Neo-Calvinism and Director of the Historical Documentation Center for Dutch Protestantism at the VU University, Amsterdam. His current fields of research are the churches in twentieth-century society, the international relations of neo-Calvinism, and the reception of Karl Barth in the Netherlands.

OLIVER O'DONOVAN was the 2008 Kuyper Prize Lecturer at Princeton Theological Seminary. Currently Professor of Christian Ethics and Practical Theology at the University of Edinburgh and a Fellow of the British Academy, he was Regius Professor of Moral and Pastoral Theology at the University of Oxford from 1982 until 2006 and is past President of the Society for the Study of Christian Ethics. His many publications include *The Desire of the Nations* (Cambridge University Press, 1996) and *Common Objects of Love* (Eerdmans, 2002).

RIMMER DE VRIES was born in the Netherlands in 1929 and studied at the Netherlands School of Economics and at Ohio State University, where he received his Ph.D. in economics in 1955. He was at the Federal Reserve Bank of New York from 1956 to 1961 and was Chief Economist and Managing Director at J. P. Morgan from 1961 to 1995.

JOHN HALSEY WOOD, JR., is a doctoral candidate in historical theology at Saint Louis University. His dissertation is provisionally titled "Going Dutch in the Modern Age: Abraham Kuyper and the Transformation of Church, Ethics, and Society in the Nineteenth-Century Netherlands," and his most recent essay is "Church, Sacrament, and Society: Abraham Kuyper's Early Baptismal Theology" *(Journal of Reformed Theology)*.

Reflections on Pluralism

Oliver O'Donovan

I

In order to think about pluralism, let us begin with the tail of the horse: the suffix "ism." One should not be tediously verbal in discussing big ideas, for language is too spontaneous and circumambulatory to be a very detailed guide to what we think. But it is interesting, all the same, that we have formed this epithet with a suffix that almost always denotes a philosophical idiosyncrasy, as in "skepticism" or "deconstructivism." As students forty years ago we would be pulled up sharply by our elders if we referred to a "pluralist" society: it was a vulgar mistake; the proper term was "plural." But intuitively we thought of pluralism as a way of seeing social relations, a perspective on them. It is not a fact that Britain is a plural/pluralist society. There are many facts underlying that assertion, some of them startling; but the proposition does not itself assert fact, but interprets it. How does it interpret it? In the first place, obviously enough, by letting the spotlight fall on social difference rather than on conformity. But the interesting thing is how it conceives this difference, which is as plurality. What is implied in understanding social difference as plurality?

Pluralism conceives difference as a danger. To raise the question of pluralism at all is to frame social reflection with anxiety. Not every difference

This is the text of Professor O'Donovan's Kuyper Prize Lecture, delivered at Princeton Theological Seminary on April 17, 2008.

would, or could, make us anxious. Linguistic difference is not alarming in itself — witness the Swiss example; neither is class difference — witness eighteenth-century England; nor even racial difference, as contemporary North America makes plain. Not every difference, then, or even an assemblage of differences, invites the construction of "pluralism." Pluralism singles out for attention something inherently worrying, which is a difference of practical principle. When sectional cultures in society act on contrary assumptions and pursue divergent courses in their relations with each other, when there are incompatible modes and expectations of public conduct, then we are anxious.

But this still fails to get to the bottom of the anxiety. The nineteenth century knew of highly differentiated societies and the dangers associated with them. Even today there is nowhere in the Western world where we begin to approach the diversity of cultural and religious plurality, with the accompanying social fragility, that prevailed in nineteenth-century India. But if you asked our colonial ancestors what the danger was, they might talk of Muslim fanaticism, Hindu superstition, Sikh persecution complex, or even Christian arrogance and incomprehension, for one may fear all these threats to a given society, and a thousand like them, without fearing what we fear in pluralism, which is a danger posed by the very constitution of society. In raising "pluralism" to a topic of discussion, we present practical difference as a foundational problem, given in the very nature of social interaction.

But then pluralism anticipates a proposal, or a family of proposals, for coping with the danger. The family likeness in these proposals is the positing of different orders of practical principles to govern conduct. If each one of us, or each community, thinks about our activity in such idiosyncratic ways that our neighbors lack all practical understanding of us, it is necessary, so it is alleged, to deploy a different kind of thinking to govern our interactions. And so there is proposed a distinction between first-order and second-order principles, the latter a regime of practical thinking detached from all fundamental principles of action — to use a term that has now become widespread, a "public reason."

But there is an odd feature about this picture: the object of anxiety and the proposal for coping with the anxiety are, in fact, one and the same: an "ideal type" of society, which is fissile, segmented, held together by principles belonging to none of its component parts. The meaning of this, I take it, is that pluralism is something rather more than a practical anxiety that anticipates a practical proposal. It is a metaphysic of society, at once a way of reading the world and a way of reacting to it. It is as though the coming of a new cultural demographics were a moment of metaphysical disclosure: an underlying reality we had overlooked became suddenly clear, and we were disillusioned of our simple idea that society is based on things held in common. It has in view something more than a modification of practice in response to determinate risks, possibilities, hopes, and fears. It has in view a conversion of disposition, enabling us to accept our ontological situation gracefully.

The proposal for a regime of "public reason" has been intensively discussed over the past quarter-century, yielding a formidable philosophical literature of considerable complexity, and any observation I make about it will inevitably be overgeneral, and probably overfamiliar. But it is necessary to review in general terms the problems inherent in the proposal if we are to throw light on the problems of the original anxiety that prompted it, what I have called "difference as plurality." The questions commonly put to public reason can be summed up as two: In what sense is it public? And in what sense is it reason?

1. The concept of the public is formed as a polar opposite to the concept of the private. You can't have public without private or private without public. But the private is defined, as the very form of the word betrays, negatively, by privation; that is to say, by walling off, excluding, refusing entry. Private thought, domestic privacy, private property, private associations, and so on are withheld from universal access. By contrast, the public is the negation of the negation, defined by the absence of barriers, by opening up, by extending communication. The public is where we venture out from our different privacies and discover what we have universally in common. Of course, public and private are not absolute opposites; they are the poles of a relative scale. A school may admit all children resident in the neighborhood as pupils, and so be "a public school," while at the same time it excludes from its premises all members of the public who are not either pupils or staff.

This phasing between the more private and the more public makes social life possible. It enables society to be organic, rather than mechanical, a living interaction of living social identities. Without the more secluded private we could have no moral identity to bring to the public realm; without the more open public we could have no use for our moral identities, no wider commonality in which they might emerge in action and reaction.

But when we look at the philosophers' "public reason" in the light of this thumbnail sketch, we find an oddity about it. This "public" seems to be constructed by privation, like another kind of private sphere. It refuses to admit moral identities formed behind its back, in private. The publicity of public reason, it appears, is less like the town square we imagine lying before our front door, more like a walled and barbed-wired garrison, bristling with warnings against entry by unauthorized personnel. It is a public conceived as another kind of privacy. But whereas the whole point of real privacy is to establish and protect identities, there is, or so it is claimed, no further identity that these inhibiting public restrictions are meant to protect.

It is, of course, essential to the general interplay of private and public that there be disciplines for making the transition from one to the other. We do not walk into the public square in bedroom slippers, nor wear an overcoat in the bedroom. Disciplines of public behavior secure possibilities for moral identities to meet. If we are to pay attention to one another, listen to one another, discuss with one another, we cannot treat one another in public with the immediacy that we use in private. Our practical principles are refracted through our various roles. A journalist conducting an interview asks questions a neighbor would never ask. A police officer inquiring about a young offender's conduct betrays no emotion at what he learns, while a parent may be expected to betray emotion. And so on. Most adults occupy many roles, public and private, and the style of behavior they adopt at any moment varies with the role. But the variations will be morally explicable, to themselves and to others, within a second-order account of how different roles require different interpretations of the same practical principles.

When public and familial responsibilities and duties of conscience converge on concrete situations, a resolution must be found that saves the essential demands of each. That means that the rules governing public conduct must be coherent with the rules governing private conduct, allowing our moral identities to encompass the stretch, so that we move between the different spheres of action without annihilating ourselves in the process. We may put the point at issue this way. Human society requires its members to sustain what Bernd Wannenwetsch has happily termed a "homologous identity," linking the performance of any individual in public and the same individual's performance in private. And that means that public disciplines, too, must arise from within the same moral traditions that shape the identities that move among the practical spheres.

Where they become separated from those traditions and absolutized, they assume the character not of disciplines, that is, aspects of an acquired wisdom, but of arbitrary prohibitions, what Foucault calls *prélèvements*. In France today a *prélèvement* is what in Britain we call a "direct debit": the money leaves the account before we have time to decide whether or not to pay it. Just so, the impositions of an absolute public reason must bypass the moral reasoning of those who participate in it. This is defended in the name of ideological neutrality, escaping the influence of any "hegemonic" tradition that might interpret the relations of human beings in ways that might be more native to some than to others. But this means it is devoid of reasons that could lead us to act. So what it presents as "second-order" reasons are in fact not reasons at all, since they do not derive from, or connect with, first-order reasons. They are simply *prélèvements*.

Christian reason will complain that this bare, stripped-down conception of public reason is devoid, above all, of charity. Charity is a hegemonic principle; that is to say, it generates not only private but also public forms of conduct, shaping a homologous identity that can move between the private and the public. If hegemonic traditions are to be expelled from society, charity, a principle born of the Christian gospel, must be expelled. And if all hegemonic traditions are to be expelled, why, in the last resort, should an exception be made for a humanist tradition of Aristotelian provenance based on distributive proportion? Unless we declare an outright prejudice for non-hegemonic principles, even that principle must quit the public square, leaving the war of all against all as the only truly pared-down, pure, and presuppositionless public order.

2. That brings us to the second question: To what extent is public reason reasonable? We speak of "practical principles" only in relation to trains of reason. Practical principles are rational dispositions; like all rational dispositions, they are culturally rooted, which is to say that they are attributes not of individuals in isolation but of whole communities and their traditions. They are not merely separate strands of reasoning, but community beliefs that generate a universe of reasons. What prompts our pluralist anxiety is the prospect of conflict between such community traditions of reasoning. September 11, 2001, would not have been half as threatening an event to the Western world if those who destroyed the World Trade Center had not been acting out of beliefs they had been taught. Our alarm was focused not on the bare fact that the perpetrators believed in what they were doing, but that they might have had reasons for believing in it, reasons deeply woven into traditions of thinking and acting in which they had been nurtured. Pluralism pits the reasons of "society" *(Gesellschaft)* in sharp opposition to the reasons of "community" *(Gemeinschaft)*. It is "foundationalist" in its account of reason, conceiving of belief systems as grounded upon posited axioms and proceeding to conclusions by deductive inference from them. Against communal reason, thus alarmingly conceived, it posits a social reason, also conceived in this positivist fashion, independent of community axiom.

Our experience as religious believers ought to tell us how wrong an account of reasoned belief this is. Religious belief does not produce moral practices deductively, like premises that produce a conclusion in a syllogism. Neither does it simply turn around in its own space, refusing questions posed to it from the world in which it lives. And what we can say about religious belief can also be said about wider, unreligious moral inquiries and convictions. Here, too, moral thought aspires to internal coherence and universality. Moral disagreement does not arise simply because individuals and communities belong to different cultures. The difference between morality and custom is precisely that morality does have universal aspirations; it refers to the place of human beings in the world, responsive to the nature of things and the will of the Creator.

Thoughtless people, it is true, fail to distinguish their customs (like eating bacon at breakfast) from their moral obligations (like protecting their children from danger). But it is the first word of moral consciousness, a word as old as civilization itself, to warn us against such thoughtlessness. A reflective culture finds its final justification of human acts outside local tradition or custom, however sacred. Moral thought conceives of action as representative. When we act conscientiously, we act as humanity, like Adam deciding for the human race as such. We recognize ourselves in others' acts, and learn about ourselves from others' acts. The good in any action I perform is never mine in a private sense; it is an aspect of the good that belongs to everybody, the human good, as it is traditionally called, since it is the goal of human action. We could perfectly well broaden that term and call it "the world's good."

Rational communication is directed to "persuasion," broadly understood — that is to say, it is concerned with communicating reasons for acting, reasons for believing, and so on. It is the means by which each of us is drawn into the perspective of other human beings, enabled to see the world through their eyes. It is an aspect of being morally capable, that we have come to be persuaded of certain things through this traditioning process. But our persuasions, though nurtured within a tradition, are not confined within its community walls. Without coercive restrictions on the movement of argument, juxtaposed communities of tradition learn from one another. There are cross-fertilizations, conversions, etc. Alasdair MacIntyre understood that fact better than most of those who have lightly taken up his talk about plural traditions.

What makes the contemporary account of reasoning unreasonable is the failure to understand or allow space for learning. Wisdom is always the object of search. And because beliefs must engage in a search to perfect themselves, because they must engage with the challenges thrown up by alternatives, disagreements may disappear as well as appear. The unstable and eclectic character of our society does not make moral agreement less likely. Since agreement in the truth is what human beings are made for, they will search for it wherever the possibility arises and we will encounter new and intriguing coalitions of thought. To free ourselves for the search, we need only to liberate ourselves from determinist theories of society that think they can tell us in advance just which agreements are, and which are not, possible.

The concept of an absolute public reason is therefore incompatible with the terms of any open practical inquiry, and especially with a Christian one. Christians may sometimes be tempted to suppose that this approach may be serviceable to the confessional and doctrinal character of their faith. But it cannot be so, for Christian confession and Christian doctrine understands itself correctly only when it understands itself as "faith seeking understanding"; Anselm's famous phrase perfectly captures the true posture of reason. Belief is itself the root and fruit of a search for God's will, and is held only in the context of such a search. It may lightly be assumed that to be open to exploration is to be hesitant about one's convictions, and vice versa; but that is actually skepticism. The one who said, "He who seeks finds," also said, "To him who has, more shall be given."

II

All this is by way of an overgeneral and perhaps overfamiliar reflection on the proposal for coping with danger, "public reason." Now we return to that diagnosis of the danger that we named difference-as-plurality.

Society is founded on plurality. Only a plurality can understand and connect themselves as *socii,* "associates." Adam in the Garden of Eden was not, and could not be, a society, since there was no associate found for him. But what kind of entity can be plural, and therefore in a position to enter into society? Entities can be plural if they can be numbered alongside one another. And entities can be numbered alongside one another if their mode of being is as individual members of a kind. We can, if we wish, count the rocks by the seashore, but our counting will be arbitrary. The pounding of the waves that broke the cliff into so many chunks and particles and granules could quite as easily have broken it into one chunk or particle or granule, or a trillion chunks or particles or granules, more or less; and it is not rock we are counting when we teach our child numbers by picking up one, or two, or three of the more conveniently sized of these pieces. Rock is not constituted in individual units. But human persons, like other animals, are constituted in units; they are essentially particular, members of their kind, and therefore in a position to enter society.

The first association, we read in Holy Scripture, was that of Adam and his wife, who was "bone of my bone, flesh of my flesh." But not only individual persons can be plural. Human communities, too, may be. An older theory of political constitution, prior to the emergence of the individualist contract-theory of Hobbes and Locke, held that political society was formed as an association of families and tribes. These units of human cohabitation could share in a society; and when they did, that society belonged to no one of them more than to any other. It was indifferently common among them.

Now, the theory we have been discussing has claimed to identify a new kind of entity among those things that can be plural, can be numbered alongside one another, and can therefore enter into association. In the phrase made famous by John Rawls, this is a "comprehensive doctrine." Rawls, though he may have invented the phrase, did not invent the idea. Heidegger in 1938 was already arguing that human knowing was constituted in modernity by the *Weltbild*, "world-picture," and that this mode of knowing must become a confrontation or struggle of world-pictures. Heidegger did not conceive this plurality as a plurality of equals. He thought that the world-picture was essentially one, that constituted by the model of scientific knowledge as "representation"; but he also thought that this one world-picture, this representational world-picture, could only establish itself eristically and so had to generate others, the medieval Christian world-picture and the classical world-picture, even though such world-pictures had never existed in their own times. A plurality of world-pictures was necessary in order for there to be one dominant world-picture.

Now confrontation and struggle are, of course, also modes of association. No two things can compete unless there is some common thing for which they compete. They must share at any rate a common view of winning or losing. Even if they strive to destroy each other, they share a common expectation of how this destruction may be effected. A competition of worldviews, then, supposes terms indifferently common to them, terms that do not belong to one of them more than to another. This association is unequal and unstable, but it is an association. And that is the logic, it seems to me, of the progression from Heidegger to Rawls. The instability of the competitive world-picture demands a stable association of plural comprehensive doctrines, just as the belligerent national-socialist society that formed

Heidegger's environment demanded the bureaucratic-juridical rights society that formed Rawls's.

I shall refer to these hypothetical intellectual entities irreverently as "isms," a reminder of the point from which we began — that "pluralism," as well as being a doctrine about isms, is also one of the kind itself. It is a reflexive doctrine of doctrines, which insinuates a view of itself and its own status into its account of the status of other doctrines. But do such entities as isms, possessing the ontological structure implied in treating them as members of a kind and in association with one another, actually exist? Do we confront here, as with a plurality of animal kinds, a basic datum of the created universe, or, as with plural languages, do we confront a fruit of providence in response to Babel? Or do we confront only an imagination? Are we dealing only with an intellectual fallacy, a version of the pathetic fallacy, which has treated human doctrines and beliefs as though they were concrete things instead of abstract?

Heidegger was right at least about the modernity of pluralism. Offered as a universal description of all societies, pluralism is easily rebutted. There are, or have been, doctrinally homogeneous societies. And indeed pluralism in this form would be self-rebutting, for the only demonstration it can have for its claim about the competing plurality of isms is to contrast modern society with older homogeneous ones. Pluralism, then, can and does answer only for a limited segment of the total social experience of mankind. It is part of that wider philosophical enterprise that attempts to account for how human existence as we know it today differs from human existence in the past. But granted this point, we see that pluralism cannot merely posit the plurality of isms. It is obliged to account for how plurality has emerged from homogeneity. How can the many isms that enter into a competitive association with one another have arisen from the "pre-ism," the homogeneous unifying doctrine that once constituted society in an age loosely described as premodern?

More clearly, perhaps, than most of those who have propounded a plurality of isms, Heidegger recognized that this question had to be answered, that pluralism could not be asserted as though it were a fact observed by journalists or statisticians. But his answer to it is a shockingly brutal one — a mere assertion of historical fiat, a philosophical strong-arm tactic. It is our fate as moderns to will our knowing as science, by representation. This form of knowing is given to us, and the reason we cannot resist it is that we cannot will not to be the subjects of our knowing. We cannot, he sternly observes, "dawdle about in the mere negating of the age. The flight into tradition . . .

can bring about nothing in itself other than self-deception and blindness in relation to the historical moment." I think there are reasons why serious democrats will have to resist that answer; and I also think there are reasons why serious Christians will have to do so. Let me, in conclusion, suggest what these reasons might be in either case.

It is clear that many defenders of pluralism think of themselves as defending democratic polity in so doing. Democratic polity depends on a strong notion of social equality, a notion extending much further than the mere admission of adult citizens to the polling booth. But equality is not a notion that can be applied independently of ontology. The question underlying every concrete decision about equality is what entities make a recognizable demand for equal treatment in this situation. (This is why a democracy that thinks of itself as independent of ontology is doomed to be the most confused age there has ever been; for it begs all its own questions, seeking to establish equality without ever having to say between what and what. Let us talk, however, of what "democrats" think, without committing them to this wild flight from ontology.) Equality is upheld within society by organs of government, and the fundamental organ of government is the court. Democracy must be, before it is anything else, a doctrine about the equality to be observed in courts of law. Courts have their own ontology. To be a subject of equal treatment in a court you have to be a "legal person," which is to say, capable of being party to a case, distinct from another legal person. Courts are impartial among legal persons.

But courts are by no means impartial among legal reasons. A court must reach a resolution of every dispute, while treating all legal persons equally. It does so precisely by treating their arguments unequally, by deciding that one set of arguments is inherently superior, and must therefore prevail. Reasons enter court in competition, that is, in an unstable association, which it is the court's business to terminate by giving effect to their inequality. Reasons enter court in order to eliminate one another. The very practice of adjudication, then, assumes that the equal respect required by legal persons cannot also be extended to legal reasons.

How, then, do isms stand before the equalizing regime of democracy? When isms confront one another in common life, they do not have to eliminate one another, and indeed usually cannot do so. If they enter court, they may do so in one of two different ways. Either they appear as legal reasons, in which case they are in no different situation from other legal reasons, or they appear as practical traditions of some community that is a party in court. When the courts are presented with isms as reasons, they are bound, as in any other case, to resolve whether they are, in terms of legal coherence, superior reasons, and so to be let stand. But when a community defined by its doctrine and practices appears before the courts, that community will have equal standing with any other legal person. The argument made recently by the archbishop of Canterbury with much controversy for introducing an element of Sharia law into British law is not an argument for doctrinal equality. It is an argument for the legal standing of communities that do in practice resolve some of their problems in the light of their doctrine. Neither in this case nor in any other can doctrines be accorded the status of legal persons, so that the apparatus of government adopts a position of indifference in respect of them. And the fact that the courts cannot give them this status explains why it is in the courts that the unfulfillable promises of pluralism for the equal treatment of all belief have been most spectacularly disappointed.

In asking why Christians will have difficulty in accepting pluralism, we must pay our respects to that great tradition of Christian pluralism derived from Abraham Kuyper, after whom this prize and this lecture are named, even while parting company from it at this point. By taking the epistemic dimension of original sin seriously, the Kuyperian theory invites us to expect deep social division at the level of "worldview" that may have to be coped with politically. And we should not, of course, ignore that advice. But there are two important questions to be asked.

Let it be admitted that the ruptures of original sin are a given in any Christian account of the moral situation of the world, and not only in the moral situation of the individual; how are we to justify the assumption that this rupture will normatively take an ideological form within society? A Christian cannot answer the question with the philosophical brutality with which Heidegger answered it: we are moderns, and therefore we cannot but will that should it be so! That strife and bitterness, the bile produced by Adam's apple, have in modern society assumed ideological forms is undeniable.

But why should this fact be more than an accident? "Sin," as Aristotle said, "is manifold." And to identify one pattern of human sin as somehow normative is paradoxical, open at least to the temptation of willing it be so. Is the Christian pluralist to play the part of the serpent in Eden, proffering the apple of ideological discord in order to bring sin, too, up to modern standards?

The second question brings me back to the point I have been circling around throughout. Why is difference of doctrine to be construed in terms of plurality? More theologically, we might ask it like this: How is the reconciling Word of God thought of as working within the ideological sphere?

The Word of God, we are told, runs swiftly. The Spirit-sent message, the promise of deliverance, the suggestion of hope — all encounter us predoctrinally before they take form within a "Christian worldview." Must this not have the effect of reconciling ideological differences and eroding the boundaries that mark the separation of plural worldviews? There is no need to think of this in terms of some big picture of the "global ecumenism" kind. The point is more modest: that in a world where the Holy Spirit is alive, we may expect to see his working in moments of reconciliation and agreement. And whereas two people whose differences are reconciled remain two people, two communities whose differences are reconciled remain two communities, it is not the case that two doctrines whose differences are reconciled remain two doctrines. That is because doctrines were never plural in the sense that people or communities are plural.

The complex intermingling of different beliefs and practices that is so typical of our culture cannot satisfactorily be thought of as a plurality of competitive isms. How, then, are we to conceive it?

Let us take the case that forms a horizon, acknowledged or unacknowledged, to a great deal of our discussion: ideological terrorism. It illustrates dramatically the thread of anxiety running through the pluralist theory, reminding us that disagreement in practical principles are never safe, but always perilous. But it also illustrates a feature of all practical principles, which is that they connect our beliefs into a chain of practical reasoning. The Islamist terrorist holds together a belief that Allah is great and a belief that innocent lives may be intentionally destroyed in pursuit of justified religious ends. For myself, I cannot help being more sympathetic to the one belief than to the other. But for him they are mutually implicated. That means that his practical principles are discursive; they take the form of a connected chain of reasoning from one point to the other. For the purposes of analysis we may itemize his separate beliefs, but in its lived texture his thought moves from one to the other to establish a connection.

There is a logic to be preserved in this movement between beliefs. Both beliefs are action-guiding, and the conduct of his life seeks a practical equilibrium that expresses both equally. There is also an order to be preserved between them. A religious belief commands a moral belief; the latter is answerable to the former, held up to question before it. And there is a universal claim implicit in his moral belief. In asserting the right and duty to conduct terrorist operations, he will maintain something as true for and on behalf of the whole world. So the validation of his beliefs is an intellectual task in which he is constantly engaged.

Once we appreciate the discursive character of moral thought, the concept of disagreement itself becomes the more complex. Presented with an isolated proposition, I can accept it or reject it outright. Presented with a series of propositions woven into a train of thought, I may find points of approximation and points of divergence. I may explore the logic of the way beliefs are held together, the implication by which they are derived. But in disagreeing I have something more to offer than a bare counterproposition. I enter into a kind of counterpoint to the train of reasoning the other is engaged in, I begin to accompany him as I challenge him and question him. I enter the sequence of his reasoned propositions, governed by a logic of moral thought from which neither he nor I can be exempt. Two people may have different viewpoints, but their different viewpoints are not two as the people that hold them are two. They are in a complex differentiation, with moments of greater distance and moments of greater proximity.

Just as public reason cannot accommodate Christian charity or Christian faith, so difference-as-plurality cannot accommodate Christian hope. Christian social theory will be known by the place it accords to mission. Mission is the work of public advocacy of the gospel in whatever form, looking for the coming of the kingdom of God, for the dawning of that universal consent to God's will in which "God shall be all in all." And that is why we may look for persuasion, conciliation, and agreement in the interim, too; but because the kingdom of God is the work of the Spirit of God, not our own work, we cannot prescribe its specific dimensions or content before the event. It is therefore an object of hope, not prediction. Christian mission in the patristic period evoked unexpected civilizational agreements, which still provide important points of reference for our own very different civilization. Responses to the gospel in our own time, too, may afford new points of social cohesion, though we do not seek them for that end alone, but as a sign of the greater unity still to come.

The Concept of "Civil Society" and Christian Social Pluralism

Jonathan Chaplin

I. The Concept of Irreducible Institutional Identity

Contemporary civil society theorizing has been fed from numerous ideologically diverse sources. Several recent studies have traced the lineage of the idea back to the eighteenth century, when the term first came to be widely circulated; or the seventeenth, when it was employed by thinkers such as Locke yet with a different meaning; or sometimes much earlier, even as far back as the Middle Ages.[1] The theories of Christian social pluralism I will be drawing on find their distant roots in medieval and early modern Christian thought, although they attain their fullest formulations only in the late nineteenth and early twentieth centuries.[2] Yet whatever story is told about the lineage of the idea, it is fair to say that most recent accounts assume that the reality of "civil society" is a distinctly modern one. The specific concepts of civil society operative within the debates of the last thirty years presuppose two fundamental and related features of modernity that came to be widely established in Europe only by the eighteenth century: the vast enlargement

1. See, e.g., John Ehrenberg, *Civil Society: The Critical History of an Idea* (New York: New York University Press, 1999).
2. For accounts of these traditions, see *Christianity and Civil Society*.

This article draws on my "Blessed Be the Tie That Binds," *Comment* (October/November 2004), http://www.wrf.ca/comment/article.cfm?ID=81, and my "Civil Society and the State: A Neo-Calvinist Perspective," in *Christianity and Civil Society: Catholic and Neo-Calvinist Perspectives*, ed. Jeanne Heffernan Schindler (Lanham, Md.: Lexington, 2008), pp. 67-96.

of the realm of individual freedom and the steady march of institutional differentiation.

Debates about the concept of civil society between the eighteenth-century emergence of the term and its late-twentieth-century revival were occasioned by attempts to come to terms with the enormous opportunities and momentous challenges thrown up by these twin developments. Classical liberal theories celebrated both of them enthusiastically. For them "civil society" was made possible by the new horizons opened up by expanded individual and institutional liberty, even though some expressed concern as to how a newly "emancipated" society could generate the moral resources necessary to sustain the new freedoms. Socialists, by contrast, while heralding industrial advances made possible by modern science and technology, and having no desire to reverse the process of differentiation, warned of the dangerous vulnerability of the new industrial working class to the atomizing thrust of modern capitalism. For Marx, "civil society" was the realm of an illusory bourgeois freedom concealing a system of proletarian enslavement. The third major ideological stream of modernity, traditionalist conservatism, shared some of the socialist critique of the atomization created by capitalism but then called nostalgically for a restoration of the organic interpersonal and interinstitutional bonds typical of medieval, or at least pre-Revolutionary, society.

Unsurprisingly, many of these concerns fed into nineteenth- and early-twentieth-century Christian social thought, as is evident to anyone reading the founding texts of Catholic and neo-Calvinist pluralism, such as Leo XIII's epochal encyclical *Rerum Novarum (RN)*[3] or Abraham Kuyper's rallying conference speech "The Social Question and the Christian Religion,"[4] both delivered in 1891. Forty years later these same concerns were summed up pointedly in the seminal 1931 encyclical of Pius XI, *Quadragesimo Anno (QA)*.[5] This document is known mainly (sometimes exclusively) for containing the first official formulation of "the principle of the

---

3. Leo XIII, "On the Rights and Duties of Capital and Labor" *(Rerum Novarum),* in *The Church Speaks to the Modern World: The Social Teachings of Leo XIII,* ed. Étienne Gilson (Garden City, N.Y: Image Books, 1954), pp. 200-244. http://www.vatican.va/holy_father/ leo_xiii/encyclicals/documents/hf_l-xiii_enc_15051891_rerum-novarum_en.html.

4. For an English translation, see James W. Skillen, ed., *Abraham Kuyper: The Problem of Poverty* (Grand Rapids: Baker; Washington, D.C.: Center for Public Justice, 1991).

5. Pius XI, *The Social Order (Quadragesimo Anno)* (London: Catholic Truth Society, 1960). http://www.vatican.va/holy_father/pius_xi/encyclicals/documents/hf_p-xi_enc_ 19310515_quadragesimo-anno_en.html.

subsidiary function of the state," but it also contains a remarkable analysis of the state of interwar European society as a whole. In it the pope sounds this classic pluralist alarm: "Things have come to such a pass through the evil of what we have termed 'individualism' that, following upon the overthrow and near extinction of that rich social life which was once highly developed through associations of various kinds, there remain virtually only individuals and the State." He went on to alert his readers to the damaging *political* consequences of this dissolution of the social fabric: "This is to the great harm of the State itself; for with a structure of social governance lost, and with the taking over of all the burdens which the wrecked associations once bore, the State has been overwhelmed and crushed by almost infinite tasks and duties" (§78).

The phrase "the loss of a structure of social governance" can stand as the common lament of social pluralists everywhere, and its restoration as their shared ambition. They warn of the disastrous fallout of a deliberate or inadvertent emasculation or suppression of the multiple social relationships, associations, communities, and institutions existing between the state and the individual — which I shall abbreviate as "institutions." Such a development actually damages all three components of society: individuals are ungrounded, undirected, and unprotected; institutions are eviscerated and corroded; and states are, as the pope put it, overburdened and overwhelmed. Contemporary social pluralists, accordingly, warmly welcomed the return of the concept of civil society to social and political theory over the last generation, because it refocused our attention on this vulnerable intermediate territory between state and individual, a territory systematically marginalized in many of the leading social and political theories of the modern age.[6]

A standard definition of civil society would resemble this one from Ernest Gellner: civil society is "that set of diverse nongovernmental institutions which is strong enough to counterbalance the state, and, while not preventing the state from fulfilling its role of keeper of the peace . . . can nevertheless prevent it from dominating and atomizing the rest of society" (Gellner 1994: 5). Elsewhere, he states that civil society is "a cluster of institutions and associations strong enough to prevent tyranny, but which are, nevertheless, entered freely rather than imposed either by birth or by awesome ritual" (Gellner 1995: 42). Equally for John Hall, civil society is "a particular

---

6. For example, Hobbes, Locke, Rousseau, Kant, Marx, Bentham, and Rawls. Montesquieu, Hegel, and Tocqueville are three leading exceptions.

form of society, appreciating social diversity and able to limit the depredations of political power" (Hall 1995: 25).[7]

A standard argument of such theorists is that a rehabilitation of the institutions of civil society is indispensable to the revival of a healthy society and polity, a necessary if not a sufficient condition. With this general proposition most Christian social pluralists would enthusiastically agree. But then it becomes extremely important to know precisely how the term "civil society" is being defined, for we need to know what kinds of institutions within it are looked to as critical sites for societal renewal, what precisely we might expect of them toward that larger goal, and what sorts of assistance they might need to fulfill those expectations. In recent debates many competing definitions of civil society have been proposed.

There has, for example, been much debate over which institutional sectors are to be included in the scope of the definition. While all agree that voluntary associations are included, and states excluded, there is disagreement on whether the family and the market are in or out. I leave that interesting debate aside here in order to concentrate on another problem in contemporary definitions, their abstractness. Note Gellner's reference to civil society as merely a "cluster of institutions and associations." This abstractness is, I suggest, one result of a common tendency in civil society thinking to view particular social institutions largely from an instrumental point of view;[8] in Gellner's case, as instrumental toward a political objective, the limitation of the power of the state. Now social pluralists of all stripes will agree that this is a worthy objective and have no objection to recognizing that strong families, neighborhoods, voluntary groups, churches, businesses, labor unions, and so forth can be effective in resisting the "control-freakery" so typical of modern states. But Christian social pluralists in particular have resisted the implication that such institutions are valuable primarily for their political functions.

Other definitions supplement such political concerns with an emphasis on the important role civil society institutions can play in taming markets or generating social capital. Don Eberly, for example, observes that such insti-

---

7. See also Charles Taylor's observation that the distinction between state and civil society "has been central to the different forms of counter-absolutist thinking" in the West. Charles Taylor, "Invoking Civil Society," in Charles Taylor, *Philosophical Arguments* (Cambridge: Harvard University Press, 1995), p. 223.

8. See James W. Skillen, "Civil Society and Human Development," in his *In Pursuit of Justice: Christian-Democratic Explorations* (Lanham, Md.: Rowman and Littlefield, 2004), pp. 19-40.

tutions "mediate between the individual and the large mega-structures of the market and the state, tempering the negative social tendencies associated with each; create important social capital; and impart democratic values and habits" (Eberly 2000: 7). Most social pluralists would agree that healthy civil society institutions help individuals acquire virtues of work, discipline, and trust that oil the wheels of society, democracy, and the economy. But Christian social pluralists in particular would, again, balk at the implication that this is their principal function. This is because they insist that the institutions of civil society can only serve wider societal, economic, or political objectives if first of all they are allowed to be themselves, to have their own unique identities publicly honored. They must be respected for what they are intrinsically if they are to be of any use instrumentally. Moreover, even if it is difficult to measure their instrumental value, they should still be free to be themselves anyway. The "structure of social governance" will not be properly restored if the institutions of civil society are not appreciated for their intrinsic contribution to human flourishing.

A key contribution to a more adequate concept of civil society, then, is the notion that institutions have "irreducible identities" — characteristic moral purposes that mark them out as *this* or *that* kind of organized, collective human endeavor. Christian social pluralists have argued that it is not enough simply to urge that there be *many* such intermediate institutions, or that they pursue *different* tasks, or that they be capable of effective *independent* action, or that they be adequately *self-governed*. It is not the mere quantity or diversity or agency of institutions that really counts but their *fittedness to constitutive human ends*. And since human beings have by creation been constituted to flourish through the pursuit of many such ends, then a corresponding plurality of qualitatively distinct institutional forms will be required to channel and structure that pursuit.

This is important to emphasize because, Christian pluralists warn, institutions can so easily be diverted from the definitive purposes they are fitted to perform. And this, surely, is especially so in a late-modern society, in which the twin and mutually sustaining forces of bureaucratization and marketization are so powerful and so penetrating, so capable of bending intermediate institutions to their own leveling imperatives. Thus, for example, the institution we call marriage is fitted to furnish a context of companionship and sexual bonding that meets human needs for intimacy and progeny, not merely to facilitate a certain arrangement of property ownership. Or, educational institutions are fitted to serve as communities of whole-person formative learning and not merely as skills-training centers to prepare for adaptation to a world of global competition. Or, political parties are fitted to orchestrate communities of political conviction and not to serve as mere electoral machines facilitating elite manipulation of a supine citizenry.

The point of insisting on something like irreducible institutional identity, then, is to summon theorists and practitioners to discern and resist the dominating, dehumanizing societal distortions of our age. To misidentify or suppress the irreducible ends of a social institution, or to conflate them with that of another, is to inhibit the flourishing of the people participating in them or influenced by them.[9] Respecting the plural irreducible identities of institutions is thus indispensable to a healthy and just human society.

To sharpen the point, compare this vision with a libertarian utopia such as that projected by Robert Nozick, one populated by a multiplicity of contractually based voluntary associations in which everyone's choices are catered to as fully as possible and coercion is supposedly reduced to a minimum (Nozick 1974: part 3). This could not begin to meet the aspirations of Christian social pluralism. It is not simply that such a model fails to do justice to the qualitative distinctions between types of human association, that voluntary associations need to be supplemented by many other kinds of institutions. The critique must, as Abraham Kuyper famously put it, be "architectonic"; it must expose the radical structural flaws in such shriveled social visions. An architectonic critique of libertarianism would argue that such a vision is actually unattainable even if it were desirable. The type of person capable of establishing and sustaining voluntary associations would simply not exist in the absence of a dense network of "nonvoluntary" institutions like the family, the church, the neighborhood, the university, perhaps the ethnic community, or the state.

The specific institutional forms fitted to enable the pursuit of what I have called constitutive human ends have been theorized in interestingly different ways by Christian social pluralists. The language of "ends" is a typi-

---

9. In a basic sense, it is true to say that institutions exist in order to serve (contribute to the flourishing of) the individual person, not that persons exist to serve institutions. As Jacques Maritain famously put it: "[The state] is an instrument in the service of man. . . . Man is by no means for the State. The State is for man" (*Man and the State* [Chicago: University of Chicago Press, 1951], p. 13). But this is a very different sense of "instrumentalism" than the one I just criticized above. In that latter sense, the problem is turning one irreducible institution into the instrument of another, which must distort the flourishing of the person in both. In Maritain's quite acceptable sense, institutions are the structured conduits necessary for the full development of the person.

cally Catholic, indeed Thomist, type of discourse.[10] In Thomist social meta-physics, each human community is conceived as naturally ordered to a specific telos, a dynamic inner tendency (guided by reason, not some irrational impulse) to realize a particular task or set of tasks, and so to contribute to the flourishing of human beings in a unique way.[11] In modern Catholic social thought, particular types of natural community have attracted special attention, notably the family, the school, the workers association, and the state, although many others have come in for extended treatment, such as the business enterprise, the professional group, or, in Catholic liberation theology, the "base community" and the political movement. A distinction is sometimes drawn between fully "natural" communities, that is, those that arise everywhere in history and are indispensable for human flourishing, and those having a more transitory existence, among which are many voluntary associations.

This is an important distinction, but it is not a distinction between communities that are rooted in the inclinations of human nature and those that are not.[12] Leo XIII, for example, designated workers associations in *RN* as "natural," even though the ones he had in mind were creatures of the nineteenth century. Such associations, he held, were specifically fitted to channel a potency deeply rooted in human nature, which we might call producer solidarity.

The strand of Catholic social pluralism springing forth from *RN*, then, proceeds from a natural law foundation. Philosopher Michael Pakaluk draws out these important implications, which clearly echo characteristic emphases in neo-Calvinist pluralism:

10. On Catholic social pluralism, see Russell Hittinger, "Social Pluralism and Subsidiarity in Catholic Social Doctrine," in *Christianity and Civil Society*, pp. 11-30; Kenneth L. Grasso, "The Subsidiary State," in *Christianity and Civil Society*, pp. 31-65. For a comparison between Catholic pluralism and the legal pluralism of Otto Von Gierke, see my "Toward a Social Pluralist Theory of Institutional Rights," *Ave Maria Law Review* 3, no. 1 (2005): 147-70.

11. Such communities are defined as either natural or supernatural, but here I comment only on the natural ones.

12. Nor does the distinction map onto a standard sociological distinction between "institutions" and "organizations" in which the former (e.g., a university) are deemed to have intrinsic purposes while the latter (e.g., a business enterprise), only extrinsic ones. In what follows I will refer to both as institutions, and suggest that both possess intrinsic purposes, as well as (sometimes) extrinsic ones. In all cases, such intrinsic purposes are given in the nature of the institution itself, not determined by external conditions or demands.

On this view, associations or communities will typically have a certain internal coherence, autonomy, and independence because of various claims and duties, binding upon their members, that arise out of the relationships and activities constitutive of those associations or communities. We can therefore speak of any association as having its own "law," formulated and administered by whichever person or persons has authority for that association, and the law of that association is appropriately based upon these claims and duties, and gets its force from them. (Pakaluk 2002: 133)[13]

What Pakaluk terms "constitutive relationships and activities" are those arising from what I have called the constitutive end of an association, its internal telos.

This Thomistic conception has been extensively analyzed and developed in twentieth-century Catholic social thought and, while less explicit in social encyclicals since Vatican II, is still at work in official teaching. There is an abundant literature, not always riveting, but sadly neglected, expounding it. Yet it is not the only conception at work in Catholic social pluralism. As Russell Hittinger has recently shown, another equally important concept has emerged, that of "participated royalty" (Hittinger 2008: 11-30). At the root of this concept is not so much a metaphysical as a theological notion, that of vocation, gift of service, or office. These terms are attempts to capture the Latin term *munus* (plural *munera*), which appears pervasively in the encyclicals, but the biblical resonance of which has been muted by it being translated rather flatly as "function" or "role." Hittinger notes that it was indeed Pope Pius XI, author of *QA*, who first began to develop the ontology of *munera*, designating not only individuals but also a wide range of institutions as bearers of *munera*: families, corporations, churches, even the state and international authorities. These institutions possessed not only rights *(iura)* but also offices *(munera)*, in which such rights were founded. *Munera*, gifted offices, are the ways in which human beings participate in the kingly quality of ruling *(regalitas)* given to them by God. To exercise a *munus*, then, is to exhibit "participated royalty." Anyone familiar with the neo-Calvinist notion of "sphere sovereignty" will immediately recognize its affinity with this notion.

Now I have so far described the organizing concepts of Catholic social pluralism without any mention of the term "subsidiarity." This principle, of-

---

13. On early Calvinist formulations of just this point, see Frederick Carney, "Associational Thought in Early Calvinism," in *Voluntary Associations,* ed. D. B. Robertson (Richmond: John Knox, 1966), pp. 39-53.

ten taken to be the conceptual hallmark of Catholic pluralism, is stated in the famous assertion in *QA* that "it is an injustice and at the same time a grave evil and disturbance of right order to assign to a greater and higher association what lesser and subordinate organizations can do" (§79). But I have been able to avoid mentioning it so far because the principle of subsidiarity is actually entirely parasitic on the social ontology I have just outlined. Subsidiarity is widely misunderstood as a mere principle of decentralization or devolution, but it does not, after all, call for all social functions to be fulfilled at *the lowest level*, but rather at *the right level;* that is, by the institution properly fitted to fulfill them. The principle itself doesn't tell us what those institutions are. It tells us that, once we have properly identified such institutions, we should assign to them, wherever possible, the functions they are fitted to fulfill. As Hittinger puts it: "subsidiarity cannot be used to settle the debates about the ontology or distribution of *munera;* rather, it is a principle governing the relations of already-distributed functions. . . . [It] is proposed as a principle of nonabsorption, not a principle that necessarily requires devolution" (Hittinger 2008: 16).[14]

So much, then, for the notion of irreducible institutional identity as this has been formulated in the discourse of Catholic social pluralism. Turning now to neo-Calvinist social pluralism, I offer four comments to bring to the fore some distinctive features of a neo-Calvinist notion of irreducible institutional identity.[15]

First, sphere sovereignty is also properly understood, not as a general principle of devolution or distribution but as a principle of nonabsorption. That which resists absorption is the divinely created identity of institutions, each dynamically spurred on by what Kuyper called its internally operative "law of life." Kuyper never produced a definitive list of what actually counted as a sovereign sphere, but from his and subsequent accounts, it is clear that the "sovereignty" of a sphere is not an end in itself but only the proper authority arising from its irreducible identity and given only to preserve and

---

14. See also Grasso, "The Subsidiary State."

15. For texts and interpretations of neo-Calvinist pluralism, see James D. Bratt, ed., *Abraham Kuyper: A Centennial Reader* (Grand Rapids: Eerdmans, 1998); Heffernan Schindler, *Christianity and Civil Society;* James W. Skillen and Rockne M. McCarthy, eds., *Political Order and the Plural Structure of Society* (Atlanta: Scholars, 1991); Peter S. Heslam, *Creating a Christian Worldview: Abraham Kuyper's Lectures on Calvinism* (Grand Rapids: Eerdmans, 1998); *Journal of Markets and Morality* 5, no. 1 (2002) (Proceedings of "A Century of Christian Social Teaching: The Legacy of Leo XIII and Abraham Kuyper," Grand Rapids, 1998); Herman Dooyeweerd, *Roots of Western Culture* (Toronto: Wedge, 1979).

protect that identity. I think the term "irreducible identity" captures this emphasis better.

Second, neo-Calvinists have insisted that diverse institutions stand to each other as ontological equals and not as ranked according to a metaphysically founded hierarchy. This claim is often asserted in polemical contrast to Thomist social theories, and it is indeed true that Catholic social thought even as late as *QA* reflects such a hierarchical model. But such a model receded into the background in Catholic social thought after Vatican II. And even some neo-Calvinists recognize a certain ranking among institutions. Herman Dooyeweerd acknowledged the important distinction between what he technically called "institutions" (such as marriage and state), which play a foundational and permanent role in society, and "associations," which are transitory and nonessential (Dooyeweerd 1945-48: 187-91). The upshot is that the difference between the two traditions on the ranking of natural communities need no longer be viewed as a significant divergence.[16]

Third, social institutions come in a wide variety of ontic types, determined by what Dooyeweerd calls their "structural principles," in which an institution's "qualifying function" plays a determining role.[17] Roy Clouser proposes the more felicitous term "structural purpose" as an alternative to "qualifying function" (Clouser 2005: 278ff.). An institution's structural purpose is what decisively shapes its irreducible institutional identity. The abstractness and complexity of Dooyeweerd's own exposition of this point can easily obscure his deeper point, which can be put quite simply. Social institutions clearly perform a multiplicity of social functions and engage in a wide and variable range of concrete tasks, but one function seems in experience to stand out in sharper relief than others in making it *this* kind of body rather than *that*. A qualifying function might be called an orchestrating function. For example, a labor union might well lay on skills-training services for its members or provide them with health insurance or act as a conduit for members' financial support of a political party, but no one supposes it has thereby become either a school or an insurance company or a political organization. These particular tasks may be perfectly legitimate, but they are (or

16. For a critique of Dooyeweerd on this point, see my "Toward a Ecumenical Social Theory: Revisiting Herman Dooyeweerd's Critique of Thomism," in *That the World May Believe: Essays on Mission and Unity in Honour of George Vandervelde,* ed. Michael W. Goheen and Margaret O'Gara (Lanham, Md.: University Press of America, 2006), pp. 215-38.

17. On Dooyeweerd's social theory, see Chaplin, "Civil Society and the State"; James W. Skillen, "The Pluralist Social Philosophy of Herman Dooyeweerd," in *Christianity and Civil Society,* pp. 97-114.

should be) subsidiary to and supportive of the union's defining purpose, which is to promote worker solidarity within business enterprises.

With this idea of a structural purpose Dooyeweerd offers an instructive refinement of the original Kuyperian intuition about irreducible institutional identity, and also provides the kind of detailed institutional analysis not typically developed to the same degree in Catholic accounts. And the point of the account is not merely classificatory, but diagnostic and critical. If, for example, a labor union becomes locked in on a permanent basis to supporting one political party, the risk is that the union either will exercise disproportionate power over the policy standpoints of that party, thus subverting the public interest, or will lack the critical distance necessary when that party's policies substantially damage its own legitimate interests. That sentence could stand as a crude summary of the troubled journey of the British trade union movement over the last two generations.

Fourth, the enduring inner nature of an institution is not seen by Kuyper or Dooyeweerd as something for which a specific design was laid out in an unfallen creation, just waiting to be stumbled upon by the sons of Adam. It is something that only swings into view over time as humans engage in the practical business of institution building in response to the numerous and unpredictable demands of history. Structural principles are to be viewed not as Platonic ideas but rather as enabling ontic conditions of historical possibility.[18] This point merits a much longer treatment than I give it here, but let me at least try to restate what I take to be Dooyeweerd's best intentions by responding to the most common line of attack directed against it.

The idea that social institutions display a structural design rooted, in some sense, in the possibilities given within created order has evoked a strongly negative reaction, some of it justified. Theological invocations of creation ordinances have, to say the least, a mixed history. Nicholas Wolterstorff speaks for many when he charges Dooyeweerd with holding a static view of institutions according to which they sport a fixed set of unchanging functions. He supposes that Dooyeweerd thinks of irreducible identities as eternal essences elevated above the vicissitudes of history. But Wolterstorff holds that there is no universal correlation between particular functions and particular institutions: "the matching up of functions . . . to

18. See Dooyeweerd, *Roots of Western Culture*, chapters 2 and 3, and Dooyeweerd, *A New Critique of Theoretical Thought*, vol. 3 (Philadelphia: Presbyterian and Reformed, 1945-58), part 2.

institutions is not to be done by asking what *the* State and *the* Business Enterprise ought to do, but by considering what *our* states and *our* business enterprises ought to do in our situation" (Wolterstorff 1984: 63).[19]

This critique has powerful intuitive appeal, and Dooyeweerd's own language often plays right into it. But I think it is based on a misunderstanding of the relationship between functions and institutions.[20] Societal functions like economic production or the raising of children or the administration of public justice are not free-floating, waiting to be picked up by just any institution. They do not get performed except by functioning institutions of particular types. Economic organizations are very bad at raising families, at any period in history. It can be plausibly argued that it is *in the very nature* of a function like, say, administering public justice that *only* something like the institution we have come to call the state can properly perform it.

This is not an esoteric point, nor one requiring gnostic insight into the Byzantine complexity of Dooyeweerd's thought. The basic intuition is straightforward. If the task of, say, administering public justice is taken on by a kinship structure like a tribe, for example, one result is likely to be that public offices will be awarded by nepotism rather than merit or election. If such a task is taken on by a business corporation, the result is likely to be something like the East India Company in which coercive public authority accrues to corporate economic power; or, perhaps, something like an oil company in a developing country that wields its own coercive private security apparatus to defend its pipelines. While the proposal to detach functions from any necessary connection with particular institutions appears, on the surface, to allow social needs to be met in a flexible, laid-back way and not according to some rigid predetermined scheme, in fact it risks undermining the proper functioning of institutions necessary to human flourishing. So what Wolterstorff calls "our" states will, like any other, need to be uniquely fitted to administer public justice if they are to do their job of protecting those vulnerable to injustice.

Whatever we make of Dooyeweerd's admittedly idiosyncratic account, my conclusion is that the basic intentions of Catholic and neo-Calvinist ac-

---

19. Here Wolterstorff relies entirely on Dooyeweerd's more popular statement in *Roots of Western Culture* and does not engage with his full philosophical treatment in *A New Critique of Theoretical Thought.*

20. For a fuller response to Wolterstorff (and a critique of Dooyeweerd), see my "Dooyeweerd's Notion of Societal Structural Principles," *Philosophia Reformata* 60 (1995): 16-36, which draws on a review of Wolterstorff's book by Paul Marshall in *Philosophia Reformata* 50 (1985): 89-93.

counts of what I am calling irreducible institutional identity converge quite closely, and together constitute a rich vein of theorizing serviceable for current reflection on civil society. The basic intuition behind this common idea can perhaps be conveyed most clearly with another example, marriage. Older Anglican marriage rites spoke, quaintly to our ears, of "the holy estate of matrimony." The term indicates that the marriage relationship is not conjured out of thin air every time a man and a woman decide to live together on a permanent basis. It is an "estate," or "office," constituted by a structured arrangement of opportunities, expectations, pleasures, obligations, and rights. Individuals enter it (or should) by choice, to be sure, but they do not arbitrarily choose the nature of the "office" into which they enter, and their "performance" as marriage partners is assessed in terms of how well they realize its constitutive purposes. The actual content of marital rights and duties, for example, allows for enormously wide variation in marital forms and behavior — yet not boundless experimentation, if the relationship is still to be called a "marriage" rather than some other, possibly in principle quite legitimate, relationship (such as friendship).

Christian social pluralism generalizes this basic intuition, holding that many social institutions, perhaps on some enthusiastic versions *all* of them, are "estates" in this sense, offices with a particular purpose and design, and a corresponding set of rights and duties. Consider now the example of the modern business enterprise. Christian pluralists don't suggest that the joint stock company can be traced back to the command to "till and keep" in the Garden of Eden. But they do suggest that the business enterprise of today is, as Wolterstorff might put it, "our" attempt to give form to the universal tendency for every society to generate "producer communities." We might define the abiding raison d'être of a producer community as the cooperative, creative, stewardly activity of producing socially needed goods or services. Once we begin to tease out what terms like "cooperative," "creative," "stewardly," or "socially needed" mean, we will inevitably find ourselves drawn into a discussion of what today we would call corporate structure, the subjective meaning of work, the priority of labor over capital (to quote John Paul II),[21] productivity and profitability, and the responsibilities of the enterprise to wider society and nature.

---

21. See John Paul II, *Laborem Exercens*, in *Proclaiming Justice and Peace: Documents from John XXIII to John Paul II*, ed. Michael Walsh and Brian Davies (London: Collins/Cafod, 1984), pp. 271-311. http://www.vatican.va/holy_father/john_paul_ii/encyclicals/documents/hf_jp-ii_enc_14091981_laborem-exercens_en.html.

Whether the joint stock company, or the transnational corporation, or the workers' cooperative, or all of the above, would emerge favorably from such discussions is an argument for another day. Christian social pluralists have, like others, sometimes fought like rats in a sack over what the irreducible identity of a particular institution is, and they still do. The point is that our choice between these and any other accounts of irreducible identity must reckon with what is most conducive to definable human needs and potentials, which are not themselves generated *de novo* by human beings, but, so Christian pluralists confess, arise from the "many-splendored wisdom" of the Creator.

II. Institutional Interconnectedness[22]

I noted earlier that modern theories of civil society take for granted the achievement of the enlarged individual and institutional freedom characteristic of modern societies. After a brief and ill-fated indulgence in nostalgic neo-medieval thought in the mid–nineteenth century, Christian social pluralism generally came to accept that this expanded realm of choice opened up new possibilities for the discharge of many important social vocations. The nineteenth century is often referred to as "the century of associations." Certainly a Christian desire to pursue new forms of social service lay behind many of the new associations (including some business associations) spawned by the demands of that century. Yet Christian pluralists were equally alert to the need for this new and fragile freedom to be balanced by a defense of, in the first instance, the church, but also of long-standing but threatened natural institutions like family or neighborhood, and by the creation of new structures of societal reintegration. They recognized that, as modern individuals and institutions had dispersed to enjoy enhanced independence from the former organic ties that had bound them, sometimes too tightly, they confronted a pressing historical imperative to put in place *new kinds of ties* that reconnected them once again in bonds of justice and solidarity. Emancipation and differentiation were spectacular cultural achievements, but, in the absence of corresponding new solidaristic ties, they carried enormous risks of personal isolation, social fragmentation, and economic injustice — risks that, of course, so

---

22. For an illuminating complementary account, see Govert Buijs, "The Promises of Civil Society" (paper presented at conference of IAPCHE, August 20-23, 2005, Moscow).

often tragically came to pass through the ravages of unrestrained industrial capitalism.

I want to give these diverse new forms of solidarity a collective name: *"interdependencies."* I use this term to indicate both that I am speaking of relationships between *genuinely autonomous* units (free individuals and differentiated institutions), and that these units nevertheless stand toward each other as *mutually dependent,* if each is to flourish. The intent is not merely to strike a balance between so-called "modern individualism" and "premodern organicism" — a simplistic contrast that, in any case, no longer stands up to historical scrutiny — but to transcend that misleading polarity, replacing it with an integrated model of persons and institutions in which individuality and solidarity are seen as mutually constitutive. Interdependencies among the institutions of civil society, I suggest, are the characteristic form of interconnection called for in a differentiated society. Supposing we designate free institutions as the "muscles" of such a society, interdependencies would then be its "sinews." We could therefore sum up one of the tragedies of modernity as this: the failure to create robust interinstitutional sinews has also meant that institutional muscles have themselves atrophied.

A pronounced focus on the irreducible identities of particular institutions has been a characteristic strength of much Christian social pluralism (which we must now irresistibly call "muscular Christianity"). This focus can serve as a valuable corrective to that type of civil society theorizing that treats qualitatively distinct institutions in an instrumental fashion. But I now want to suggest that a more concerted focus on interdependencies is also required if Christian social pluralism is to make a satisfactory contribution to contemporary civil society theorizing.

Christian pluralism has, of course, already had a good deal to say about interdependencies. Consider neo-Calvinism first. It is often not noticed, especially among Kuyper's North American readers, that he himself regularly invoked organic metaphors to speak of the close interconnections among the various institutions of society (metaphors that were at times couched unhelpfully in the Romantic language of the nation and its parts). Yet Kuyper was animated mainly by a desire to secure the independence of institutions against external threat rather than to explore their complex interdependencies with each other. Dooyeweerd had much more to say about interdependencies, and spoke of the importance of new "integrating" processes to balance those of "individualization" and "differentiation," processes he regarded as historically legitimate yet radically incomplete in themselves. Among these were many kinds of "interlinkages" emerging in modern society among differentiated institutions.[23] And among these interlinkages was a specific type, enkaptic interlacements, in which an unusually close bond was established between different types of institution, which I think we can properly call a specific "bond of service." My notion of interdependency is really an attempt to restate in less complex and hopefully more appealing terms the central intent behind these various notions. To do so I need the help of a sister tradition.

Catholic social thought has certainly addressed the theme of interdependencies extensively under its interrelated conceptions of the organic harmony of society, of a common good that overarches and integrates the partial goods of lesser communities, and, more recently, of the norm of "solidarity" that is to be realized not only within communities but also between them.

Neo-Calvinists have often displayed an allergic reaction to these more integrative notions, due to their apparent vulnerability to statist or corporatist interpretations. For example, consider the capacious definition of the common good formulated in *Mater et Magister (MM):* "the sum total of those conditions of social living, whereby men are enabled more fully and more readily to achieve their own perfection" (§65).[24] When the promotion of such an all-embracing societal project is then carelessly attributed to the state, some neo-Calvinists mutter darkly about the danger of "collectivism" or even "totalitarianism." On closer inspection, however, it becomes clear that such utterances as this one in *MM,* infelicitous though they may be, must be read alongside the powerful countertendencies in Catholic social thought considered earlier, which are radically antitotalitarian.

Leaving that dispute aside, let me explore further one of the resources in Catholic social thought: the way in which the principle of subsidiarity *itself* discloses a profound understanding of institutional interdependencies. Recall the formulation of the principle in *QA:* "it is an injustice and at the same time a grave evil and disturbance of right order to assign to a greater and higher association what lesser and subordinate organizations can do." The sentence immediately following is just as important: "For every social activity ought of its very nature to furnish help *(subsidium)* to the members of

23. The term is a stand-in for a very long Dutch construction appearing in Dooyeweerd's technical account of these integrating processes. See Dooyeweerd, *A New Critique,* vol. 3, part 2 (chapter 5), and part 3 (chapter 2).

24. In Walsh and Davies, *Proclaiming Justice and Peace,* pp. 1-44. Also available at http://www.vatican.va/holy_father/john_xxiii/encyclicals/documents/hf_j-xxiii_enc_15051961_mater_en.html.

the body social, and never destroy or absorb them" (§79). This statement alludes to the Thomist notion that humans are naturally social and cannot realize their ends in isolation, needing the help *(subsidium)* of society in order to do so. In a deep sense, Catholic social thought regards *society as a whole* as performing a subsidiary function in relation to persons and institutions. As Pius XII puts it, "all social activity is of its nature subsidiary."[25] And this, in fact, turns out to be another way of saying that the particular good of persons and lesser communities cannot be realized apart from what is supplied by the common good. Hence, as twentieth-century Catholic social philosopher Johannes Messner succinctly puts it: "the law of subsidiary function and the law of the common good are, in substance, identical" (Messner 1949: 196).

If this reading of the principle of subsidiarity is valid, it mandates a correction to the standard application. It is common to suppose that, as a leading Catholic commentary puts it, "subsidiarity only looks one way" (Calvez and Perrin 1961: 332) — namely, from the state downward. This vertical reading of the principle is not wrong, but the deeper intent I have tried to draw out from it also suggests a horizontal, or indeed multidirectional, application. For if all social activity is subsidiary, then all social institutions need not only to protect their irreducible identity, but also to look beyond themselves and offer "help" or service to others. The form of service they offer will reflect their irreducible identity. Each will nurture the gifts *(munera)* with which it has been entrusted and make them available to institutions that need them. And they will do so not, in the first instance, by launching some program of external outreach, but simply by being themselves. Conversely, then, each institution is dependent upon the unique forms of service only other institutions can supply. Multisided institutional interdependency is constitutive of a human society reflecting the design of the Creator.

A consideration of Dooyeweerd's notion of enkaptic interlacement leads to the same conclusion. For Dooyeweerd, an enkaptic interlacement occurs when one institution makes its unique functions available for use by another, as when, for instance, churches "offer" their liturgical functions to the state when acting as a public registrar of marriages; or when a political party in a parliamentary system "offers" its internal unity of conviction to the state in order to organize a government. An enkaptic interlacement is, as I read it, a case of one-way functional subservience. Now these are interest-

---

25. Quoted in J.-Y. Calvez and J. Perrin, *The Church and Social Justice* (Chicago: Henry Regnery, 1961), p. 122.

ing cases of interinstitutional service, but I see no reason why we should confine the analysis to instances of one-way subservice. I suggest we extend it to embrace all and any case of interinstitutional functional service, so bringing us to the same point we arrived at following my earlier reformulation of the principle of subsidiarity.

I need to emphasize that the notion of interdependencies is not simply a descriptive concept, a mere fact about a modern society. The creation of appropriate interdependencies is a normative vocation, one responding to a characteristic vulnerability of a society marked by advanced individualization and differentiation. So we need to speak of the normative character of interdependencies, and to spell out precisely which forms of mutual dependence are appropriate and which destructive. A lot of detailed analysis is required here, but the general principle is clear: institutions should see to it that the kinds of interdependency into which they are drawn or which they seek out allow for the *mutual* flourishing of irreducible identities. Clearly many existing interdependencies are inherently antinormative, while others, legitimate in themselves, cause either unilateral, bilateral, or multilateral decay.[26] Interdependencies can and do easily slide into unhealthy *dependencies* that damage the weaker party (as in radically asymmetrical labor contracts), or drag both sides into a downward spiral of degenerate *codependency* (as with what Eisenhower famously called the "military-industrial complex").[27]

The market is an obvious site today of labyrinthine interdependencies, both healthy and unhealthy. Generalized dismissals of "free markets" miss the point that, for example, workers need businesses to supply jobs, consumers need businesses to supply products, governments need businesses to generate tax revenues. Equally, however, those who romanticize "free markets" tend to overlook that businesses are equally dependent on robust families, schools, health-care institutions, welfare service providers, public transport networks, regulatory frameworks, and many other things provided by the state. The growing recognition of what is called the "social embeddedness" of markets captures well this general claim about interde-

26. I would approach the problem of what has been called "uncivil society" — where civil society institutions come to damage rather than support personal liberty and public virtue — under the heading of interdependencies that have become unhealthy dependencies.

27. This general claim is helpfully earthed in concrete public policy analysis by Stanley Carlson-Thies, who calls for a model that recognizes both "true identity" and "appropriate partnership" between government and educational or welfare organizations. See his "Why Should Washington, DC, Listen to Rome or Geneva about Public Policy for Civil Society?" in *Christianity and Civil Society*, pp. 165-87.

pendencies.[28] Yet as we know all too well, such networks of unavoidable mutual dependency create many openings for exploitation or other forms of domination, as was evident in the predatory preregulated labor markets of the nineteenth century, and as has been seen in the dangerously deregulated global financial markets that brought the world to the brink of systemic collapse in late 2008.

My argument, then, suggests the inclusion of the market within a reformulated definition of civil society. Building the market into a definition of the scope of civil society encourages analysts explicitly to name the complex and often hugely influential interdependencies present in markets and to critically assess their health. Where illicit market forces compromise the integrity of institutions like families, neighborhoods, or universities, etc., or the universal dependency of all human institutions on the natural environment, civil society theorists will want to urge a reining in of such forces rather than simply a carving out of spaces of immunity from them. Placing market relationships within the category of interdependencies is a way of insisting that they, too, are subject to the controlling norm of mutual flourishing; that markets are, as the cliché quite rightly has it, servants, not masters.

So it turns out, after all, that social usefulness is not a supplement to irreducible identity but an intrinsic part of it. This is the truth that "instrumentalist" theories of civil society seek but fail to grasp because they lack a sufficiently rich social ontology of irreducible institutional identity and normative interdependencies. It is, I suggest, intrinsic to the irreducible identity of all institutions that they offer unique types of service to others. This, at least, is one opening gambit in thinking about how Christian social pluralism can enrich and correct civil society theorizing today.

References

Calvez, Jean-Yves, and Jacques Perrin. 1961. *The Church and Social Justice.* Chicago: Henry Regnery.

Clouser, Roy. 2005. *The Myth of Neutrality.* Rev. ed. Notre Dame, Ind.: University of Notre Dame Press.

Dooyeweerd, Herman. 1945-48. *A New Critique of Theoretical Thought.* Vol. 3. Philadelphia: Presbyterian and Reformed.

28. See Bob Goudzwaard, *Capitalism and Progress* (Grand Rapids: Eerdmans, 1979); Herman E. Daly and John B. Cobb, *For the Common Good* (Boston: Beacon Press, 1994).

Eberly, Don E., ed. 2000. *The Essential Civil Society Reader: The Classic Essays.* Lanham, Md.: Rowman and Littlefield.

Gellner, Ernest. 1994. *Conditions of Liberty: Civil Society and Its Rivals.* New York: Penguin.

———. 1995. "The Importance of Being Modular." In *Civil Society: Theory, History, Comparison,* edited by John A. Hall. London: Polity Press.

Hall, John. 1995. "In Search of Civil Society." In *Civil Society: Theory, History, Comparison,* edited by John A. Hall. London: Polity Press.

Hittinger, Russell. 2008. "Social Pluralism and Subsidiarity in Catholic Social Doctrine." In *Christianity and Civil Society: Catholic and Neo-Calvinist Perspectives,* edited by Jeanne Heffernan Schindler. Lanham, Md.: Lexington.

Messner, Johannes. 1949. *Social Ethics.* St. Louis and London: B. Herder.

Nozick, Robert. 1974. *Anarchy, State, and Utopia.* Oxford: Blackwell.

Pakaluk, Michael. 2002. "Natural Law and Civil Society." In *Alternative Conceptions of Civil Society,* edited by Simone Chambers and Will Kymlicka. Princeton: Princeton University Press.

Wolterstorff, Nicholas. 1984. *Until Justice and Peace Embrace.* Grand Rapids: Eerdmans.

Sphere Sovereignty among Abraham Kuyper's Other Political Theories

James D. Bratt

I

"Sphere Sovereignty" was probably the most memorable speech Abraham Kuyper delivered over a long lifetime of notable orations. Its occasion was the founding of the Free University, which he saw as the linchpin of his life's work. Here would be formed a leadership class to give his movement a permanent presence on the national scene; from here would flow a coherent body of distinctively Christian scholarship to defend and advance the claims of faith on the cultural high ground where so much of modern life was shaped. For both of these reasons — sociological and intellectual — the ontology of human life that Kuyper alludes to in the speech, the theory of sphere sovereignty, has launched a thousand ships. It was to "sphere sovereignty" that his activist followers would regularly appeal in warranting their policy proposals, and it was in the exploration of the spheres that the academics in his train would find an agenda for research as well as a charter for creative innovation.[1]

---

1. The speech was originally published on the date of its delivery, October 20, 1880, as *Souvereiniteit in Eigen Kring* (Amsterdam: J. H. Kruyt, 1880). The full text (except for its extensive ceremonial postscript) is available in English as "Sphere Sovereignty," in *Abraham Kuyper: A Centennial Reader*, ed. James D. Bratt (Grand Rapids: Eerdmans, 1998), pp. 461-90. The fullest study of sphere sovereignty as a theory is J. D. Dengerink, *Critisch-historisch onderzoek naar de sociologische ontwikkeling van het beginsel der "souvereiniteit in eigen kring" in de 19e en 20e eeuw* (Kampen: Kok, 1948). For shorter, English-language analyses, see Bob Goudzwaard, "Christian Social Thought in the Dutch Neo-Calvinist Tradition," in *Reli-*

It is remarkable, then, to note how very brief is the allusion to the spheres themselves in Kuyper's speech: little more than one page of the nineteen that the modern English text entails. The picture was imprecise as well. For instance, as to the number of spheres, Kuyper says that "there are as many . . . as there are constellations in the sky." He names "a domain of the personal, a domain of nature, of the household, of science, of social and ecclesiastical life," but then lists another seven and yet another three before and after this enumeration. As for how we should picture these domains, they might be "'spheres,' each animated with its own spirit," Kuyper says, but they also might be "cogwheels" in a "great machine . . . spring-driven on their own axles." The image doesn't matter, he hurries on, so long as we remember that "the circumference of each has been drawn on a fixed radius from the center of a unique principle" (Kuyper 1998b: 467). In short, just as his evocation of the spheres is not a major part of Kuyper's speech, it is only the barest beginnings of a social philosophy.

What is it, then? As the above citations indicate, "Sphere Sovereignty" reads like the poetic effusions of a bard. The oration covers a vast terrain and accomplishes a great deal of work there, and in relatively brief compass, by pouring forth a rich sequence of images and allusions, draping them over a scaffolding that takes some effort for us to discern. We have to work even harder to locate the core assumptions at work in it. But the speech works all the better for that; its aim was to inspire, and among those inspired was Herman Dooyeweerd, who, fifty years later, would elaborate Kuyper's suggestions into a systematic philosophy of being and human action.[2] "Sphere Sovereignty" worked more immediately, too, as a piece of political philosophy; in fact, by quantitative measure, this was a prime intent of the speech. But again, it is political philosophy told as historical narration, a heroic narrative of world history in which ultimate values were at stake and in whose culminating act the small band of believers whom Kuyper was addressing were to play a vital role. The speech's other prime focus is epistemology, where Kuyper sketches out an alternative model of perception and interpretation that is all the richer for being embedded in cultural or social-psychological context (Kuyper 1998b: 481-88). This paper will bypass that as-

---

gion, Economics, and Social Thought, ed. Walter Block and Irving Hexham (Vancouver: Fraser Institute, 1986), and James W. Skillen and Rockne M. McCarthy, eds., *Political Order and the Plural Structure of Society* (Atlanta: Scholars, 1991).

2. Herman Dooyeweerd, *De Wijsbegeerte der Wetsidee,* 3 vols. (Amsterdam: H. J. Paris, 1935-), translated into English as *A New Critique of Theoretical Thought,* 4 vols. (Philadelphia: Presbyterian and Reformed, 1953-58).

pect to focus on the speech's political theory, comparing it to themes Kuyper laid out on two other seminal occasions, one earlier and one much later in his career. If sphere sovereignty as a theory of social ontology is typically used with a political subtext, that fits with its original intent. But how does it fit with the political theory Kuyper delivered in other circumstances?

II

The first occasion occurred seven years before, when Kuyper went out on the Dutch university lecture circuit late in the election season of 1873 to recruit young leaders for the budding political party he wanted to build. Such a purpose required some theoretical, at least rhetorical, fireworks. On the other hand, the public could expect some reference to that year being the twenty-fifth anniversary of the Dutch Constitution of 1848, but for that monument Kuyper's constituency had little affection. His solution was to ignore the Constitution altogether and pursue the source of constitutionalism instead, and his title indicates where he found it: "Calvinism, the Source and Stronghold of Our Constitutional Liberties."[3] Kuyper took pains to spell out that this "Calvinism" included its theological particulars, not just the generic Reformation that his mentor Guilliame Groen van Prinsterer favored for political grounding. Further unlike Groen, who was a historian much given to the markers of Netherlandic tradition, Kuyper's address bypassed the Netherlands altogether to range through the annals of international Calvinism, and invoked precedents that Groen at a comparable age would have found deeply troubling. Kuyper's culminating line would return to local, party recruitment purposes: "I hope . . . that at least the young people of the Netherlands will not echo the old libel . . . that we, Dutch Calvinists, are a party of reaction!" (Kuyper 1998a: 317). But to get there he had to suppress his audience's and his mentor's reflex antipathy for political revolution. The speech does deliver an argument for stability and order, but it gets there through a history of resistance, rebellion, and revolution — good, Christian revolution.

The Calvinist particulars at the bottom of Kuyper's speech were the absolute sovereignty of God and the pervasiveness of human sin.[4] Far from

---

3. Most of the text is available in English in Bratt, *Abraham Kuyper*, pp. 279-317. It was originally published as *Het Calvinisme, oorsprong en waarborg onzer constitutioneele vrijheden* (Amsterdam: B. van der Land, 1874).

4. He spells them out on pp. 307-10 in the text.

warranting monarchy, as Restoration Catholic and Lutheran theorists had argued, Kuyper insisted that these tenets pointed toward a republic. On the first point, divine majesty brooked no human imitation; republicanism was the political counterpart of iconoclasm, both being rooted in the Calvinist horror of idolatry. On the second point, of human depravity, while monarchs did seem particularly prone to that condition, Kuyper jibed (invoking Calvin to boot), "he [Calvin] also knows that the same sin pervades the masses and that, as a result, there will be no end to resistance and rebellion, mutiny and troubles, except for a just constitution that restrains abuse of authority, sets limits, and offers the people a natural protection against lust for power and arbitrariness" (310). Quite contrary to Groen, then, who deemed Calvin a monarchist who had reluctantly accommodated to Geneva's republicanism, Kuyper insisted that, "given a free choice, Calvin certainly prefers the republic" (304-6).[5] There followed a quick two-step that took him even further from his mentor. The doctrine of divine election, which Groen typically skirted lest it arouse dissension in Dutch Protestant ranks, Kuyper invoked as the charter for "the democratic form of church government" with clear implications for civil government as well (309-10). With its leveling effect upon all human pretension, the doctrine of election made democracy safe for Calvinism; with the moral discipline against self-seeking it bred in the believer, it made Calvinists safe for democracy.

It was not theology but historical narrative that did most of the work in this speech, however, so the case studies Kuyper chose were telling. He took them up in reverse chronological order, beginning with the United States as the paragon of liberty and of Christian sobriety, moving thence back to English Puritanism, before crossing the Channel to the French Huguenots and then across the Swiss border to Geneva. There Calvin in his generation connected predestination to democracy while Theodore Beza, in the next, justified Huguenot armed resistance during the French wars of religion. Theirs was *a constitutional* resistance to *tyrants*, Kuyper reminded his hearers, but it entailed a violent defiance that Groen, for one, could never endorse. Groen had supplied Kuyper with the writings of Edmund Burke to help him prepare this lecture, but when Kuyper came back and asked for the Huguenot sources as well, Groen revealingly replied that he did not have them in his library.[6] In the lecture itself Kuyper emphasized that the authors in question

---

5. Quotation on p. 305.

6. See Groen's letter to Kuyper of September 2, 1872, in A. Goslinga, ed., *Briefwisseling van Mr. G. Groen van Prinsterer met Dr. A. Kuyper, 1864-1876* (Kampen: Kok, 1937), pp. 194-

— Beza, François Hotman, and Hubert Languet (probably Philippe du Plessis-Mornay) — limited the right of resistance to duly constituted leaders, the "lesser magistrates," and subsequent historians have confirmed the significance of their concept for the development of modern political theory.[7] Yet, in chronicling the French case, Kuyper had to refer to a rebellion persistent, systematic, bloody, and radicalizing enough to count as a revolution, save for its lack of success. The case of seventeenth-century English Puritanism was not thus limited. That the Puritan Revolution involved violent insurrection, regicide, destruction of church properties, terror in the (Irish) countryside, instability eventuating in military dictatorship, and any number of other features resembling the French Revolution Kuyper did not mention. For him the Puritans' was a permissible, even commendable, revolution as attested by its documents and the good discipline of Cromwell's New Model army (296-97).

Kuyper could bypass these uncomfortable parts of this story because in both the Huguenot and Puritan cases he gave substantial attention to ecclesiastical rather than to civil politics. This reflected the centrality for him of religious freedom among other "constitutional liberties," but it also served his current polemical agenda; when he gave his talk, his proposals for reforming church arrangements in Amsterdam, where he still served as a parish pastor, had just been rejected (Vree 2000: 42-44, 46, 54-58). Thus his lecture attributed the synodical hierarchy that so frustrated him in the Netherlands back to the Huguenots' adoption of it as a political necessity in the face of military emergency. He hurried on to laud the English Independents for boldly and properly adapting "the Calvinist principle" to their own time and place over against their Presbyterian opponents, who had tried to import the alien French system on the assumption that "Calvinism was a petrifaction, bound to the form it had assumed, take it or leave it." In this battle, Kuyper concluded, the Independents had not only the greater success but the clearer claim on Calvin, "who had unambiguously rejected the idea

---

95. Jan W. Sap, *Paving the Way for Revolution: Calvinism and the Struggle for a Democratic Constitutional State* (Amsterdam: VU Uitgeverij, 2001), critically notes Groen's aversion to Huguenot resistance theory, pp. 294-95.

7. Huguenot resistance theory is well laid out in Julian H. Franklin, ed., *Constitutionalism and Resistance in the Sixteenth Century: Three Treatises* (New York: Pegasus, 1969). Quentin Skinner traces its development and significance in *The Foundations of Modern Political Thought*, vol. 2 (New York: Cambridge University Press, 1978), pp. 239-348, as does John Witte in *The Reformation of Rights: Law, Religion, and Human Rights in Early Modern Calvinism* (Cambridge: Cambridge University Press, 2007).

that one should be tied to an established form." By this argument Kuyper's ideal of a "circle of free, autonomous congregations" bound on a "voluntary, not coerced, relationship with the synod" received the imprimatur of Calvin himself. Likewise the "separation of church and state," which — according to Kuyper — Puritans in old England and New had the virtue to realize, followed "necessarily" from "Calvinistic principle" (Kuyper 1998a: 293-301).[8]

The New England case allowed Kuyper to return to civil politics proper, and with the happiest prospects for his thesis. No one could deny that "modern liberties flourish in America without restriction" or that "the people of the Union bear a clear-cut Christian stamp more than any other nation on earth." This was not a coincidental but a causal relationship, Kuyper argued, rooted in the nation's Puritan origins. Kuyper had plenty of sources for this casual conflation of "New England" and "America," since the standard histories of the time (and for several more generations) exercised the same assumption. At the same time, his characteristic organic sociology was at work. Whatever the cultural complexity and the numbers on the ground that made it an exceptional minority by 1776, New England still represented "the core of the nation"; and whatever might have developed over the subsequent century via westward movement, civil war, and industrialization, the original Puritan stamp still held on America's core convictions and collective character. To make this claim credible, however, Kuyper's "Calvinism" now had to leave behind any confessional particulars (he includes Wesleyans in the mix!) and take on enough elasticity to become a broadly cultural pattern of moral earnestness, healthy enterprise, middle-class discipline, and public respect for religion (286-92).[9] So arranged, he could hammer home his point: the best of modern liberties were the fruit not of the French Revolution but of Calvinism.

He put it to the students before him with a flourish: "We are Antirevolutionaries not because we reject the fruits of the revolutionary era but because, history book in hand, we dare contest the paternity of these good things. With much evil the revolution also brought Europe much good, but this was stolen fruit, ripened on the stem of Calvinism under the nurturing warmth of our martyrs' faith, first in our own land [which he now

8. Quotations on pp. 293, 294, 306, 300.
9. Quotations on pp. 286, 289. The method and mistakes of Kuyper's appropriation of American history are detailed in James D. Bratt, "Abraham Kuyper, American History, and the Tensions of Neo-Calvinism," in *Sharing the Reformed Tradition: The Dutch–North American Exchange, 1846-1996*, ed. George Harinck Krabbendam and Hans Krabbendam (Amsterdam, 1996).

substituted for the Huguenot case he had detailed in the narrative], then in England, and subsequently in America." Kuyper had to acknowledge ruefully that in Europe "what had been refused from the hand of Calvinism was eagerly accepted from the hands of the French heroes of freedom." Yet it would not do to accept that surrogate for, along with "Calvinistic liberties . . . [the Revolution] introduced a system, a catechism, a doctrine; and this system, running counter to God and his righteousness, destroys the bonds of law and order, undermines the foundations of society, gives free play to passion, and gives the lower realm rule over the spirit." Put positively, only Calvinism supplies "the moral element," "the heroic faith," and those intermediate institutions that over the years had become the proper extension of the "lesser magistrates"; all of these, and only these, together give order to liberty and so assure its perpetuation (298-99, 313, 314, 312). In sum, Kuyper sees political constitutionalism as the fruit of Calvinist revolution.

III

Seven years later, in the autumn of 1880, Kuyper returned to some of these themes in "Sphere Sovereignty." Now he was not speaking at other universities but founding his own. He was speaking from the chancel of the cathedral of Dutch Protestantism, Amsterdam's Nieuwe Kerk, but speaking on behalf of the humble believers in the land who had seemingly been bypassed by time and power. Yet for this group Kuyper was now staking a claim to prospective social and cultural power. His speech needed to be insurrectionary, then, to announce possible reversals in the status hierarchy; at the same time, it had to build for the long run, laying out an ontological order that was both dynamic and stable. The leaders who would be minted at the new university would be asserting their own religiously distinctive claims, yet would play responsibly on the public stage, working for the common good. Befitting these thematic tensions, the very title of the talk in Dutch is ambiguous — does "Souvereiniteit in Eigen Kring" mean sovereignty in *its* sphere, or sovereignty is *our* sphere? The text unmistakably develops both meanings. Its topic is sovereignty, its phobia is tyranny, its passion is freedom, its premise is order. It rehearses the familiar conjunction of divine election with democracy, and across these formal "principles" runs a quick survey of world history, of national history, of the history of the Dutch Reformation and Réveil, all of them intertwined.

Kuyper showed his purpose for "Sphere Sovereignty" by evoking at the earliest opportunity the controlling trope of early-modern political philosophy: absolute and undivided sovereignty. Since French Calvinist resistance had been both the occasion and the victim of that assertion, Kuyper placed such sovereignty out of human reach in God's hands alone, from whence it was refracted into any number of localized human sovereignties. These were not to be regathered into one, Kuyper insisted, until Christ returned in majesty at the final judgment. Any human pretension to claim unitary sovereignty was thus blasphemous on the face of it and bound to wreak woe in practice; this in fact, Kuyper the bard recounted, was the grim thread of world history, from the tyranny of the Caesars to the persecutions of the Hapsburgs, Bourbons, and Stuarts, to the contemporary scene where universalistic claims of revolutionary popular sovereignty on one side matched Hegelian elevations of "the State as 'the immanent God'" on the other (Kuyper 1998b: 469-71).[10] Historically, the antidote to these assaults had been constitutional restrictions on the centralization or exercise of power, particularly the separation and balance of powers as theorized by Montesquieu and ensconced in the United States Constitution. But Kuyper entirely bypassed constitutional measures on this occasion. Rather, he postulated discrete and autonomous spheres of human life to replicate on the ontological level the separation and balance of powers in politics. Not on paper or in formal offices, then, but in the divinely given creation and the evolution of organic societies lay the most promising grounds of resistance to the unitary beast.

For all its theocentric claims about the nature of being and for all its occasion of founding an integrally, distinctively Christian university, "Sphere Sovereignty" proceeds with very modest biblical evidence and a minimum of theological elaboration. Again Kuyper appeals to history, but now to a different set of examples and by a different method than was true of his earlier address. Put colloquially, in "Sphere Sovereignty" the villains command the historical highlights; its march is the parade of the unitary beast, contested by valiant yet faltering heroes of liberty. The Netherlands — with the Sea Beggars and hedge-preachers, the Reformation and Réveil — now casts up more of the resistance than in "Calvinism and Constitutional Liberties," but altogether they hardly make a convincing case for the theoretical plausibility or future chances of the harmonious constellation of spheres that Kuyper lauded. The strongest precedent his account can muster on this front is an evocation of "that glorious life, crowned with nobility," that marked the late-

10. Quotation on p. 466.

medieval Low Countries, "exhibiting in the ever richer organism of guilds and orders and free communities all the energy and glory that sphere sovereignty implies" (470).

Why had no theoretician arisen to explain and warrant the virtues of this order? One had, and on a Calvinistic basis at that! This was Johannes Althusius, author of the definitive compendium of Calvinist, antiroyalist thought (*Politica Methodice Digesta,* 1603) and syndic of Emden in the first quarter of the seventeenth century when that city was "the Geneva of the North," a strong influence on the emerging Dutch republic and its Reformed church.[11] Indeed, by his writing, civic, and ecclesiastical roles, Althusius qualifies in some historians' estimation as the John Calvin of Emden. His consociational political theory intentionally answered Jean Bodin's theory of unitary sovereignty. It also chartered something very like Kuyper's society of sovereign spheres. In Althusius's thought, human nature is indelibly associational, thus precluding individualism from the start and making communities the building blocks of societies. So also Kuyper's social ontology begins: "Our human life . . . is so structured that the individual exists only in groups, and only in such groups can the whole become manifest" (467).

Each human association, Althusius continues, was empowered by its original purpose to flourish but was also bound by the inherent limits of that purpose so as not to intrude on others — be it another cluster in the same or in an adjoining domain of human activity. Certain powers were delegated upward to the next tier of human interaction by decision of the smaller units, which units (not the individuals in them) remained the constituent members of these broader bodies. Thus, individuals were members of households, the heads of which delegated some of their political power to town councillors who in turn appointed mayors and syndics. For economic purposes, citizens joined guilds; for religious purposes, churches; for recreation, clubs. Successive intermediate levels of association then conveyed authority up the scale of more general gatherings: towns constituted a province, provinces a nation, nations an empire. Human society was thus a pyramid of association where power remained as close to the base as possible, in which no one at any level ruled without the consent of the governed, in which different functions of human life developed freely according to the

---

11. On Althusius, I have relied on the introduction by Frederick S. Carney and preface by Carl J. Friedrich to Carney's translation of Althusius's *Politics* (Boston: Beacon Press, 1964), and on James W. Skillen, "The Political Theory of Johannes Althusius," *Philosophia Reformata* 39 (1974): 170-90.

purposes of that function and not to the call of another, and in which responsible decisions remained closest to those most competent to make and implement them. Moreover, authorities in every domain and at every level were constrained by the laws divine and natural that set norms for that association; thus, individuals within a consociation — the father in the home, guild A in the town economy, province X in the nation — could be disciplined by their fellows or, if need be, by their superiors, for violating their trust.

A more friendly and auspicious antecedent for sphere sovereignty could hardly be imagined. Why did Kuyper not invoke it? Jonathan Chaplin suggests that Althusius had been rendered suspicious for Kuyper by the work of Otto von Gierke, a close contemporary of Kuyper (born 1841) who, in a book published in the same year as "Sphere Sovereignty," completed his harnessing of Althusius to the evolution of the German constitutional state that he deemed the final synthesis in the inherent dialectic between "fellowship" and "lordship," community and sovereignty, that drove German history.[12] As von Gierke celebrated the newly fashioned German Empire as the ultimate synthesis between French libertarianism and Russian autocracy, Althusius thus became associated with what Kuyper deemed a grim danger. Methodologically, moreover, von Gierke had secularized Althusius to make his process of human association entirely immanent in its drive and court of appeal. To this explanation we need to add an inference of some psychological discomfort on Kuyper's part. By 1880 "Emden" would raise strong cross-pressures in his mind. It was, after all, the home of Johannes á Lasco, upon whom Kuyper had written the prizewinning paper that made his academic name already in graduate school. In that essay, however, Kuyper had very pointedly and repeatedly championed á Lasco's ecclesiology over that of Calvin — a thesis that well served the purposes of the Groningen theological faculty that had sponsored the essay contest. The Groningen school's cultural nationalism and liberalizing theology yearned for native Netherlandic sources to vaunt against the narrow dogmatism of the "French ideologue" from Geneva whose Flemish followers had poured into the future republic during the war

---

12. On von Gierke, see Antony Black's editor's introduction to Otto von Gierke, *Community in Historical Perspective: A Translation of Selections from Das Deutsche Genossenschaftsrecht* [1881], trans. Mary Fischer, ed. Antony Black (Cambridge and New York: Cambridge University Press, 1990), pp. xiv-xxx. Von Gierke published *Johannes Althusius und die Entwicklung der naturrechtlichen Staatstheorien* in 1878. Jonathan Chaplin explains Kuyper's aversion to Althusius via von Gierke in a personal communication to the author, November 4, 2003.

for independence, blighting Dutch tolerance in the process.[13] Groningen thus championed Erasmus, Arminius, and Grotius as native Dutch spirits. But Kuyper in the years since writing that treatise had turned resolutely Calvinist in theology, making it embarrassing to valorize Emden for civil as well as ecclesiastical government.

We must also return to our original observation. What is political theory, named as social ontology and told as historical narrative, doing in a speech that charters a university? The answer lies in the very strong evocation in "Sphere Sovereignty" of a basic tenet of republican political philosophy, that virtue is the bulwark of liberty. The antidote to centralizing unitary power is not just spheres orbiting in theoretical sovereignty but in a resolute citizenry whose moral strength animates the spheres with vitality enough to resist the encroaching power. And before that, Kuyper emphasizes, to resist the deterioration *within* a sphere — particularly the oppression and abuse of power that its leaders visit upon the weaker — which invites the state into that sphere's domain: more accurately, which requires the state to undertake its divinely given calling to redress abuse of power and reestablish justice. It is self-discipline and self-sacrifice by the people in their respective roles that preclude and withstand statist intervention. But such moral rigor depends much upon morale; if we would fight the sloth and corruption that ultimately lead to oppression, Kuyper repeats, we need hope to live a better way. We need a vision contrary to that vended by the hegemonic threat. In other words, the core of political resistance and the road to social flourishing lie in culture. There the university can and must serve the crucial role (468, 473-77). For Kuyper the Free University was to flesh out a robust worldview over against that of the materialist hegemon that was stalking Europe, a worldview that would make of a faithful Reformed remnant a collective player equal in strength — perhaps one day, superior in allure — to the forces animated by secularist naturalism. At the same time, the scholars at the university would be conducting the advanced research on pressing problems of modern life needed to articulate alternative policies from a Christian point of view. "Sphere Sovereignty" charters a mandate and arena for Christian public intellectuals.

13. On this context see Jasper Vree, *Abraham Kuyper's Commentatio (1860): The Young Kuyper about Calvin, a Lasco, and the Church*, vol. 1 (Leiden: Brill, 2005), pp. 9-12.

IV

In that light it is striking to read the animadversions toward academics as public intellectuals that Kuyper vented on a later occasion. This happened in 1908 — well after Kuyper's vision had birthed a complex of institutions that were beginning to realize significant success. The Free University, where Kuyper had taught for twenty years, was now expanding its faculty and student body across a broader range of disciplines. Its graduates were moving up the ranks of the professions, and its clientele was fruitfully engaged in the discussion and application of the writings on the arts, economics, theology, and politics that the faculty had duly put forth. The Antirevolutionary Party (ARP) had increased its numbers, seen some of its policy proposals enacted into law, and was currently in charge of the government for the third time. Kuyper was still in command of the party as chair of its Central Committee and as editor of its newspaper, *De Standaard.* But in this third Antirevolutionary (AR) cabinet he was not prime minister, and party members had other newspapers to read as well, some of them voicing pointed critiques of his leadership. Those critiques were also being sounded in party councils by the rising generation of leaders. In fact, that cohort conducted something of a coup in maneuvering through an unexpected set of circumstances to take over the government in 1908, pointedly keeping Kuyper out of the cabinet. In this context Kuyper published a series of articles entitled "Our Instinctive Life" that laid out a third distinct view of politics and its ontological footing.[14] It championed charismatic leadership and its organic bonds with the popular will.

Kuyper begins this account by extolling the instinctive powers of the animal world. This was his "fable of the bees" — more accurately, of the spiders, for whom he shows a fascination comparable to Jonathan Edwards's two hundred years before. The wisdom of the insects partakes of the wisdom of God, Kuyper continues; even more so does the practical intelligence, the knack and knowledge, of ordinary people. In marked contrast to the raptures about frontline scholarship that he proclaimed in "Sphere Sovereignty," Kuyper now characterizes knowledge gained by "reflection," by book study, to be "artificial" and passing. The "perfect" knowledge we shall have in

---

14. *Ons Instinctieve Leven* appeared in book form (Amsterdam: W. Kirchner, 1908) after its original newspaper run earlier that year. For the context of its controversy, see Dirk Th. Kuiper, *De Voormannen: een social-wetenschappelijke studie* (Meppel: Boom, 1972), pp. 245-51 and 345-47.

the next world as promised by 1 Corinthians 13 will be "spontaneous, imme-diate, and completed at once" — quite more like the practical intuition of everyday life than like the abstract schematizing of academics (Kuyper 1908: 257-59).[15]

We can recognize here an old theme in Kuyper, one sounded already in his first major cultural address some forty years before, "Uniformity, the Curse of Modern Life." But it was also newly current, part of a whole stream of vitalist complaints being sounded left, right, and center, on both sides of the Atlantic, in the early twentieth century.[16] Bourgeois civilization with its iron laws of science and industry, its fixed routines of city life and business management, was crushing the unique and the spirited, blighting the indi-vidual and the race, draining the life force and imagination, corroding both the animal virtues and the noblest callings that had made human life worth living. Kuyper repeated these complaints. Amidst the urban and urbane withered the rich color and variety of traditional rural life; under advancing civilization, the collective wisdom that had passed down the generations was giving way to the "calculated," to the "pedestrian and prosaic, the measured and formal." Such routinization was even creeping into the ARP, and inevita-bly so, Kuyper allowed. But that tendency had to be vigilantly guarded against lest the holy cause succumb to "spiritual decline and emotional im-poverishment" (268).

As we shall see, Kuyper had a very practical objective in view in publish-ing this polemic, but he was also addressing a problem of modern popular movements for which Max Weber and Georges Sorel were drawing up their respective prescriptions at much the same time. In Weberian terms, Kuyper intended to fight the passage from charismatic to bureaucratic authority as much and as long as he could. To that end he defended the mode of proce-dure he had built into the party from the start over against a new one that the AR Young Turks were proposing to institute. They wished, first, to make policy formation more collaborative, to open study and discussion clubs for all party members, led by men in the junior ranks, so that the means as well as the ends of AR initiatives would be democratic. They also proposed to

15. Quotations on p. 258.

16. "Uniformity" is available in English translation in Bratt, *Abraham Kuyper*, pp. 19-44. It originally appeared as *Eenvormigheid: De Vloek van het Modern Leven* (Amsterdam: H. de Hoogh, 1869). Of many studies of the discontents of modernity, see J. W. Burrow, *The Crisis of Reason: European Thought, 1848-1914* (New Haven: Yale University Press, 2000), and T. J. Jackson Lears, *No Place of Grace: Antimodernism and the Transformation of American Cul-ture, 1880-1920* (New York: Pantheon, 1981).

bring trained competence to bear more heavily in policy formulations and parliamentary workings — that is, to replace the too general and too simple pronouncements of the clergy sector of party leadership with the trained expertise of lawyers and social scientists (Kuiper 1972: 246-47).[17] The rising leaders advocating these changes were, let us remember, men trained at Kuyper's university and practicing the mandate he had given them: to conduct the close research into modern problems needed to give general AR principles real purchase on the ground.

This Kuyper now scotched. There are three kinds of people in the world, he declared: the large mass of folk who live by practical wisdom, the few genuine scholars whose all-absorbing studies take them to the depths of things, and then the jabbering class of the superficially learned, textbook-trained in secondhand knowledge, who prided themselves as being above but lacked the virtues of the other two groups. The professionals who were most likely to escape this hazard, to have "brought the instinctive and the reflective life into a higher synthesis," Kuyper continued, were in fact the clergy, whose duties in the pulpit sent them back every week to the fonts of deep knowledge and whose parish duties exposed them every day to the intimate life of ordinary folk. The derivative "amphibians" now contesting for leadership knew not the real life of those they invited to the policy table; otherwise they would know how mistaken their suggestions must be. For Kuyper, lauding the commoners, also reminded them of the "boundaries" that demarcated their "sphere." Having intuitional knowledge, they neither could nor would really wish to take part in policy formation. If confronted with rival formulations, the role of "the non-learned public" was "to use its own instinctive life as touchstone and for the rest to rely on its leaders" (Kuyper 1908: 263, 267-68).[18]

That connection needed to be vibrant and heartfelt, however. This, for all his appeals to custom and tradition, Kuyper sensed to be the modern in politics and the key to his own success. Writing entirely in the third person and in innocently vague language, he lays out in these articles the two roads to his reign. In the series' preliminary discussion of instinctive gifts, where he locates the artist — indeed "all true *talent,* and especially all *genius*" — Kuyper describes how a charismatic speaker operates, and in so doing leaves a self-portrait that was confirmed by any number of observers: he "takes up his position before the gathering, feels the contact between his spirit and

---

17. Kuyper alludes to the proposals satirically in *Ons Instinctieve Leven*, pp. 270-71.
18. Quotations on pp. 267-68.

that of his audience, and opens the tap. Almost automatically the words begin to flow, the thoughts leap out, the images frolic — psychological art in action. This is even more true of the *genius*. He does not plod and pick away at things; he does not split hairs or prime the pump. . . . By spiritual X-ray vision he sees through doors and walls and virtually without effort grasps the pearl for which others grope in vain" (260). Thus there is in Kuyper's typology a fourth category of person besides the earlier three of commoner, scholar, and derivative intellectual — there is the genius, and it is he who lifts up and weaves together policy proposals, social studies, political theory, and tactical considerations into an eloquent statement that accords precisely with "what they themselves [the common voters] instinctively felt in essence" (267). That leadership common people value far more than a spot on a study committee, Kuyper averred.

Charisma cannot remain just occasional in the contests of modern politics, however. It has to be ensconced in ordinary party work without getting routinized. Kuyper explained how to meet this challenge by having recourse to another French source — not to Calvin or the resistance theorists this time but to Gustav Le Bon and his work on the psychology of the crowd.[19] Written out of long, skeptical retrospect upon the French revolutionary tradition, Le Bon's description of how the crowd becomes a being in itself, with its own will and mind sweeping up those of its individual members, becomes for Kuyper a theoretical warrant for the Antirevolutionary delegate assemblies — party conventions — that he had instituted and were held at the peak of every biennial election season. At these meetings the lonely village delegate comes to know that he is part of a vibrant, national movement, Kuyper explains. A written statement of principles becomes a living conviction. A campaign platform becomes the staircase to a better tomorrow. No doubt the oratory of genius had its part in the drama. But drama it had to be. A party "must have the means — as the *psychology of the crowd* demands — to convert sober realism into enthusiasm, cool calculation into holy passion. . . . It is by virtue of the power and animation that radiates from these meetings that we have become who we are." Technical expertise — and on this note Kuyper concluded his series — is the armor of Saul in God's good fight, but the intuitive bond connecting the leader genius with the faithful is the stone of David that fells the giant (275-77).[20]

---

19. Kuyper cites and develops the theme of Le Bon's *La psychologie de foule* (Paris: F. Alcan, 1895) on pp. 264-66.

20. Quotation on pp. 276-77.

Kuyper was a bard who laid out his political theory in historical narratives. The first of these warranted revolution led by lesser magistrates on constitutional grounds. The second called forth intellectual visionaries to invigorate mediating institutions. The third celebrated the organic bond between the charismatic leader and popular consciousness. The second part of this triad, that laid out as sphere sovereignty, can become — and did become in Dutch neo-Calvinist history — routinized into place-holding conservatism. The other two notes must be heard as well to grasp Kuyper's full vision and the magic of his inspiration. Revolution and charisma are dangerous quantities, of course, and it is sphere sovereignty's job to discipline them. But it is also necessary for sphere sovereignty to be enlivened by their fervor and hope.

References

Kuiper, Dirk Th. 1972. *De Voormannen: een social-wetenschappelijke studie.* Meppel: Boom.

Kuyper, Abraham. 1908. *Ons Instinctieve Leven.* Amsterdam: W. Kirchner.

———. 1998a. "Calvinism: Source and Stronghold of Our Constitutional Liberties." In *Abraham Kuyper: A Centennial Reader,* edited by James D. Bratt. Grand Rapids: Eerdmans.

———. 1998b. "Sphere Sovereignty." In *Abraham Kuyper: A Centennial Reader,* edited by James D. Bratt. Grand Rapids: Eerdmans. Originally published as *Souvereiniteit in Eigen Kring.* Amsterdam: J. H. Kruy, 1880.

Vree, Jasper. 2000. *Abraham Kuyper als Amsterdams predikant (1870-1874).* Amsterdam: HDC.

Kuyper, Neo-Calvinism, and
Contemporary Political Philosophy

Gordon Graham

I

In the third of his Princeton *Lectures on Calvinism* — "Calvinism and Politics" — Abraham Kuyper boldly asserts that "no political scheme has ever become dominant which was not founded in a specific religious or antireligious conception" (Kuyper 1931: 78). By this single assertion Kuyper places a large gulf between his position and that of contemporary political philosophy, at least in the mainstream liberal-democratic tradition. Dominated by the towering figure of John Rawls, contemporary political philosophy expressly divorces political justice from all comprehensive conceptions of life, whether religious or antireligious. As Rawls puts it: "A conception of justice is political when it is presented independently of any wider comprehensive religious or philosophical doctrine" (Rawls 1993: 223). "This means," he continues, "that in discussing constitutional essentials and matters of basic justice we are not to appeal to comprehensive religious and philosophical doctrines — to what we as individuals or members of associations see as the whole truth" (225). In sharp contrast, Kuyper's ambition precisely is to discuss constitutional essentials in the light of a comprehensive religious doctrine that he, as an individual, firmly holds to be "the whole truth."

Given their diametrically opposed starting points, what should we say about the relation between Kuyper's neo-Calvinist political vision and contemporary political philosophy? There are a number of possible answers. First, we could discount Kuyper as a conversation partner for political philosophy in the early twenty-first century just because time has passed and important historical changes have occurred. His world, in short, is not ours. Rawls himself alludes to something like this attitude in defense of his strictly political conception of a well-ordered society. He remarks that "the diversity of reasonable religious, philosophical, and moral doctrines found in democratic societies is a permanent feature of the public culture and not a mere historical condition soon to pass away. . . . Our exercise of political power is proper and hence justifiable only when it is exercised in accordance with a constitution the essentials of which *all* citizens may reasonably be expected to endorse in the light of principles and ideals acceptable to them as reasonable and rational" (216-17, emphasis added).

Kuyper's appeal to the Calvinist worldview in explanation of the proper and justifiable exercise of political power inevitably fails to meet this condition, for the simple reason that the vast majority of modern citizens are not Calvinists. The political world of 2008 is quite different from that of 1898, and thus not a world to which we should expect Kuyper's lectures to speak.

Such a response, of course, presupposes what many would claim to be false — that Kuyper's world was less pluralistic than ours. He was, after all, reaffirming the merits of the Calvinistic worldview precisely because so many rivals had entered the field. With this fact in mind, it is not implausible to hold that value pluralism is a feature of the *self-image* more than the *reality* of the present age. In any case, merely pointing to historical change is insufficient to warrant us in discounting Kuyper. His claim is in part about the *viability* of political schemes — what makes political ideas command allegiance and thus have impact in the real world of politics. If Kuyper is right in this, then Rawls is simply wrong in his speculation that diversity of religious, moral, and philosophical doctrines is a permanent feature of public culture. One implication we might draw from this is that the sort of liberalism whose credibility relies on the phenomenon of cultural diversity is in fact much more vulnerable to change than Rawls's optimistic assertion implies. And here, indeed, we find an important resonance with a thought to which the emergence of fundamentalist Islam has led — namely, that the liberal optimism of the 1980s is indeed misplaced. Contra Francis Fukuyama, we are nowhere near the end of history or the last man.

In any case, historical debate about the moral diversity of times past, and speculation about its cultural permanence, does not get to the heart of the disagreement between Kuyper and contemporary political philosophy. Kuyper believes something more than is strictly asserted in the sentence I quoted; he believes not only that comprehensive religious or antireligious doctrines have greater political impact, he also believes that they provide a better theoretical grounding for social order than any limited conception of public reason (such as Rawls advocates) can provide. His aim in the Princeton lectures, of course, is to show that Calvinism is the best of all such doctrines, but in terms of the conflict with contemporary political philosophy this is a secondary matter. Equally secondary, it seems to me, is the fact that in developing his fundamental conception of "public reason" based on "overlapping consensus" Rawls came to rest more and more of his case on the historical contingencies of European political history. The spirit of liberalism more broadly considered, and to which Rawls gives a specific articulation, affirms the superiority of a certain kind of moral neutrality in politics, over against Calvinists, communists, natural law theorists, and so forth, quite generally and irrespective of the particularities of history and geography. The real debate between the two positions, therefore, centers on a philosophical thesis: Are political institutions and practices best grounded in a comprehensive worldview like Calvinism, or should any such worldview be eschewed in the name of political liberty?

Unfortunately, if this is indeed a full account of the dispute, the debate between Kuyper and contemporary political philosophy does not promise much in the way of novelty or illumination. That is because over the last three decades or more, the merits and demerits of the kind of political neutrality modern liberalism espouses have been debated ad nauseam, and since almost everything that anyone can think of saying has been said, it is implausible to suppose that revisiting Kuyper would add much. However, my purpose in this paper is to argue that the concept of "sphere sovereignty," which is such a distinctive feature of Kuyper's political thought, does have something new and important to contribute to contemporary political philosophy. To appreciate what this is, though, we need to set the issue in a rather wider context.

II

A common understanding of the very broad sweep of European political history holds that until relatively recently all political societies could be divided into two classes — the rulers and the ruled. Of course, a society of any complexity will always generate a "middle" class of administrators, tax collectors, and bureaucrats of one kind or another, and this may be a very extensive class, as it was in the Babylonian Empire. But the members of any such middle class can nonetheless be seen to fall on the side of "the ruled."

Their existence did not alter the underlying political structure in which any rights and freedoms the ruled might enjoy were bestowed by the authority of the ruler, while the ruler's own entitlements to wealth and power derived from elsewhere — conquest, lineage, or divine appointment perhaps.

According to this same general picture, a number of widely different influences and historical events eventually brought about a radical change in the relationship of ruler to ruled to the point of a complete reversal. It is this reversal that John Locke articulates in his *Second Treatise of Civil Government,* arguably the founding document of political liberalism. Rulers were now understood to owe their authority to the ruled, and could legitimately use coercion only insofar as it was derived from a "social contract" by which "the people" transferred their natural rights to self-defense and retributive punishment to "the magistrate." There thus comes into theoretical existence a properly "liberal" state, an institution of coercive power, whose authority is derived from the prepolitical rights of those subject to it, and whose sole independent justification is efficacy in the protection of these rights.

Locke speaks, a little vaguely, as though "the contract" were a one-off event in the distant past. Serious critical difficulties soon surface for this supposition. When was the contract made? Even if this question could be answered satisfactorily, it would remain unclear how agreements among past generations could create political relationships binding on present persons who were not party to those agreements. Locke's answer is to augment the historical conception with an "idealized" contract to which citizens give "tacit" consent simply in virtue of living in and benefiting from society. It is this idea that Hume subjects to devastating criticism in "Of the Original Contract." The renewal of a social compact between rulers and ruled through repeated democratic electoral mandates is widely thought to address these criticisms. In this way a philosophical alliance is forged between liberalism and democracy, an alliance so powerful that nowadays the two terms invariably appear in each other's company. Democratic institutions provide the means by which individual human rights form both a basis for and a check on the use of coercive political power.

Something like this is the historical/conceptual backdrop against which another prominent contemporary political philosopher — Jürgen Habermas — advances his conception of "the public sphere." He characterizes this as "a domain of our social life in which such a thing as public opinion can be formed" (Habermas 1997: 105). The public sphere is the locus of journalists and political activists, but it is not the exclusive preserve of such people. Any and every citizen can occupy the public sphere, including citizens who hold political office, so long as they are dealing "with matters of general interest without being subject to coercion" (105).

The introduction of the public sphere between rulers and ruled thus gives rise to a three-level social or political structure.

> In the first modern constitutions the sections listing basic rights provide an image of the liberal model of the public sphere: they guarantee society as a sphere of private autonomy; opposite stands a public power limited to a few functions; between the two spheres, as it were, stands the domain of private persons who have come together to form a public and who, as citizens of the state, mediate the state with the needs of bourgeois society, in order, as the idea goes, to thus convert political authority to "rational" authority in the medium of the public sphere. (107)

We may leave aside here (admittedly important) questions about the general accuracy or inaccuracy of this very broad historical sketch. What matters for present purposes is the three-level conception of social and political life that has resulted from it. In the confrontation between personal autonomy and political power, or the individual and the state, or freedom and authority, stands the public sphere. Its mediation between these opposites has two crucial aspects. First, it is free from coercion. Second, this is what ensures that debate within it can result in the right kind of consensus, one that legitimates the exercise of state power.

Is the public sphere, so conceived, a sovereign sphere? This question is crucial to its being an effective buffer between individual freedom and state power. By asking it, we bring Kuyper's distinctive concept of "sphere sovereignty" into contact with a leading idea in contemporary political philosophy — the consensus of the public sphere. The two concepts might be brought closer still if we suppose that "the public sphere" encompasses all those spheres to which Kuyper was inclined to attribute sovereignty — the church, the arts, education, and economics, for example. For the moment, though, let us concentrate on the more general question: Is the public sphere a sovereign sphere?

III

It is useful to characterize the public sphere in these terms. A genuine public sphere exists in any society that enjoys free speech, a free press, and other media; open access to public office; and freedom to form or oppose political parties. We should add further that none of these activities or institutions is directly subject to coercive political control. So characterized, it seems that the existence of a public sphere is virtually definitive of a free society, and if it is, it must therefore be described as a sovereign sphere. However, this appearance is deceptive, and its deceptive character is evident once we see that such a public sphere is wholly compatible with what I shall call a "statist" society.

A statist society can be characterized as one in which all actions judged to be socially beneficial are undertaken directly or indirectly by the state and paid for out of general taxation. In the real world these generally include the administration of justice, internal security, public safety, schooling, medical services, and basic welfare programs, but increasingly they have been extended to include state-sponsored "public education" in, for instance, adopting healthy lifestyles; rejecting all forms of discrimination based on race, sexuality, or gender; and encouraging reuse and recycling. Increasingly too, the institutions of science, art, culture, and even sport look to the state for political and financial support. Such support is usually formed and guided by policy, often drafted by think tanks that include academic and social researchers. These policies then form the basis of election manifestos by politicians competing for office, and thus (theoretically at least) provide the focus for debate within the public sphere.

Now it is perfectly possible, and in many places a reality, that all these aspects of social life should be entirely under the control of the state. Consider the case of schooling. It is not hard to imagine circumstances in which the education of children from infancy to adulthood is governed by a standard, government-approved curriculum and provided free of charge either in schools directly managed by agencies of the state, or under license by private state-accredited organizations that are subject to regular processes of inspection. It takes no very great effort of imagination to extend this picture to most other social institutions — hospitals and clinics, sporting academies, art museums, research laboratories, and so on. The crucial point to stress, however, is that we are not thereby imagining the totalitarian world of Stalinist rule. Something very like this condition exists, in fact, in most modern democracies. The difference with Soviet Russia is not the extent of the state's involvement in the life of the society, but the existence of a real public sphere. However, such a public sphere does not function as a barrier to incursions by the state into the life of the individual. Its role is to subject statist policies to free and open discussion. Indeed, it might plausibly be suggested that a vibrant public sphere positively encourages large-scale expansion in the range of topics to which political policy statements are devoted, since any suggestion that some topics be excluded from discussion in the public sphere is easily represented as a denial of freedom within it.

It follows, I think, that the public sphere, though a sphere of freedom, is not itself a sovereign sphere. Even when it functions exactly as it ought to, it offers no protection to those areas of life that the Kuyperian holds to be sovereign spheres — which for present purposes (leaving the notable cases of economics and the family aside) I shall take to be art, education, science, and religion. Religion might be thought to be a striking exception to the general trend I have been describing since in modern democracies the state (for the most part at least) does not attempt to replace the church or regulate its spiritual activities. It is often for this reason, I think, that liberal political philosophy takes the position of religion to be the touchstone of a free society. Yet there is a good case to be made for thinking that the state's indifference to the church is a result of the church's declining significance as a social institution, and the freedom accorded to religious believers is a reflection of the increasingly widespread view that religious belief is a matter of purely personal practice and preference, no more socially consequential than a preference for football over baseball. The mark of a society in which political governance is importantly *limited* would be one in which some areas of life that are deemed to be *of great importance* are nevertheless areas about which political policy documents are silent — in short, a society in which there truly are sovereign spheres.

Liberal democratic political theory may not have generated statism as I have defined it, but by pinning its hopes on the freedom of the public sphere, it can do nothing to contain it. Alone amongst social institutions, the state claims a legitimate monopoly on coercion. It is for this reason that its growth at the expense of all other social institutions, and its increasing involvement even in the minutiae of family and private life, is to be regarded as a prima facie threat to freedom. If, as I have been arguing, the liberal public sphere, however vibrant, cannot counterbalance the state in this regard, we need some alternative theoretical resource. It is here, as it seems to me, that Kuyper's political vision and contemporary political philosophy come into their most rewarding contact, and here that we can make most effective appeal to the concept of "sphere sovereignty."

IV

To call a sphere other than the state "sovereign" is to say that it ought to be impervious to political intrusion by the actions and officers of the state even when these have been sanctioned by full, fair, and free political processes.

> The family, business, science, art and so forth are all social spheres which do not owe their existence to the state, and which do not derive the law of their life from the superiority of the state, but obey a high authority within their own bosom; an authority which rules, by the grace of God, just as the sovereignty of the State does.
>
> This involves the antithesis between State and Society, but [it is] upon this condition [that we] honor in each of these parts the independent character which appertains to them.
>
> In this independent character a special higher authority is of necessity involved and this highest authority we intentionally call sovereignty in the individual social spheres, in order that it may be sharply and decidedly expressed that these different developments of social life have nothing above themselves but God, and that the State cannot intrude here, and has nothing to command in their domain. This is the deeply interesting question of our civil liberties. (Kuyper 1931: 90-91)

Kuyper's list of sovereign spheres is imprecise, but for present purposes this does not matter. Of greater importance is the theoretical underpinning that he gives them. It has several dimensions that would warrant closer examination, but I shall focus on just two. First, a sovereign sphere has its own source of final authority, and second, political direction can accomplish nothing within the sphere.

In illustration of these points it is helpful to think about universities as institutions of learning, institutions with which Kuyper himself was particularly concerned, of course. In awarding degrees as well as other academic accolades, a university uniquely determines what is of intellectual worth. This is not to say that it always gets it right, only that there is no other authority to which anyone can meaningfully appeal. Furthermore, though coercion may successfully command the *trappings* of scholarship and learning, it can accomplish nothing *real* in this sphere. No public policy, however well intentioned and well funded, can make it the case that universities subject to it will produce new and innovative intellectual work. Precisely the same sort of argument can be mounted in defense of the sovereignty of the religious and artistic spheres. All these instances allow us to assert the general principle that a sovereign sphere exists wherever there is a distinctive aspect of social life for which such an argument can be made.

Any such argument, of course, need make no mention of a further important aspect of Kuyper's contention — that "these different developments of social life have nothing above themselves but God." In defending the independence of academic authority along the lines suggested, we do not have to say anything about the ultimate sovereignty of God. There is, however, a further interesting step to be taken. For Kuyper, the sovereignty of God with respect to these spheres (as also the sphere of politics into which the church ought not to intrude) is connected with the "important significance of the Calvinistic doctrine of 'common grace' [which teaches that] all the liberal arts are gifts which God imparts promiscuously to believers and unbelievers" (Kuyper 1931: 160). Contemporary political philosophy has a secular counterpart to Kuyper's common grace — the equal moral worth of all human beings — and a related substitute for the sovereignty of God over all things, namely, the sovereignty of "the people."

This modern substitute for the authority of God is expressly distilled in the familiar slogan *Vox populi, vox Dei* — the voice of the people is the voice of God, a slogan whose spirit is at work in democratic theory even when these precise words are not used. Though the triumph of the democratic ideal is relatively recent, the expression is an ancient one. Its earliest use, however, makes a point directly contrary to the democratic ideal. In a letter dated A.D. 798 Alcuin, adviser to Charlemagne, writes: "Those people should not be listened to who keep saying the voice of the people is the voice of God, since the riotousness of the crowd is always very close to madness." When modern democrats use the same expression in a positive spirit, they are not thinking of the riotousness of the crowd, of course, but of the orderliness of the ballot box in the exercise of universal suffrage. Even so, there is still point in asking this question. What exactly is it (to repeat Habermas's phrase) that enables the voice of "the people" to "convert political authority to 'rational' authority"?

God, let us agree, is the fount of wisdom and justice. It is this that makes his authority binding on rational agents such as we may take human beings to be. We ought to do what God bids us, because his will is certain to be in accord with the best and wisest course of action. Kuyper sees, rightly, that this cannot be taken as a warrant for theocracy in politics, since the voice of the theocrat is a human, not a divine, voice. The theoretical point remains, however. God's sovereignty is grounded in his wisdom and justice. That is what gives us reason to acknowledge it. In what, theoretically, is the sovereignty of the people grounded?

The answer has to lie with some appeal to consensus. Even if we disregard questions about the important distinction between consensus and simple majority opinion, this problem remains. There is no guarantee that a consensus fairly and freely arrived at will constitute a convergence on the true or the rational. History and experience demonstrate that a consensus can form around policies and actions that are unjust and unwise. A process of public deliberation untainted by intimidation or manipulation can nonetheless lead to consensual agreements that are detrimental to public welfare, to the rights of the individual, or to the conservation of scarce resources. When this happens, rational agents are under no obligation to follow the consensus. But democracy bids them do so. This was, in fact, Plato's objection to democracy, and it remains unanswered, I think. As long as it does so, what follows is that the will of the people can express a majority in favor of political coercion, but unlike the will of God, it is quite unable to "convert political authority to 'rational' authority."

The conclusion to be drawn is this: Kuyper bases his political philosophy on a worldview that accords sovereignty to a number of social spheres, of which government and politics is only one. He denies politics any preeminence on the grounds that the sovereignty specific to it has no authority over the other spheres, which derive their sovereignty directly from God. By contrast, the main stream of contemporary philosophy eschews all such worldviews as the ground for political arrangements, and places its faith in a public sphere where properly public reason can be freely exercised. On closer examination, however, the sovereignty of the liberal public sphere is revealed as illusory. There is nothing in its proper functioning that limits state power and thus secures it as a sovereign sphere. Furthermore, the additional invocation of democracy as the mark of legitimacy displaces political judgment with political opinion and thus gives preference to the irrational over the rational, provided only that the former can command a majority consensus. In short, the liberal democratic public sphere offers no special protection for either freedom or reason. It is against the background of this conclusion that the attractiveness of a much more robust conception of sphere sovereignty, something like that which Kuyper espouses, becomes evident. If this means that political philosophy must reopen theological questions, then so be it.

References

Fukuyama, Francis. 1992. *The End of History and the Last Man.* New York: Free Press.

Graham, Gordon. 2002. *The Case against the Democratic State.* Exeter: Imprint Academic.

Habermas, Jürgen. 1997. *"The Public Sphere" in Contemporary Political Philosophy.* Edited by Robert E. Goodin and Philip Pettit. Oxford: Blackwell.

Hume, David. 1741-2/1963. "Of the Original Contract." In *Essays Moral, Political, and Literary.* Oxford: Oxford University Press.

Kuyper, Abraham. 1931. *Lectures on Calvinism.* Grand Rapids: Eerdmans.

Locke, John. 1690/1960. *Two Treatises of Government.* Edited by Peter Laslett. Cambridge: Cambridge University Press.

Rawls, John. 1972. *A Theory of Justice.* Oxford and New York: Oxford University Press.

————. 1993. *Political Liberalism.* New York: Columbia University Press.

Kuyper, Sphere Sovereignty, and the Possibility of Political Friendship

Michael J. DeMoor

I. The Idea(l) of Political Friendship

This paper makes use of a term that can seem alternately an anachronism or a straightforward oxymoron: "political friendship." I want to suggest that this concept has a vital role to play in pluralistic democracies and thus should have a place in political thinking that draws on Kuyper's Christian democratic pluralism. However, I ought to begin by characterizing the meaning and significance of political friendship.

The idea of political friendship implies first that the state is a kind of *community*. Though it has an institutional and legal expression, it is at heart a society of persons — conceived in this case as *citizens* — rather than a set of structures, procedures, or positive laws. Moreover, the state on this view is to be thought of as a *moral community*, one held together by a shared vision of and participation in (some aspect of) the good life. Thus for Aristotle, the political community is the highest expression of the life of active virtue and hence the perfection of other moral communities (the family and the village in particular). In participation in the political community — that is, in active citizenship — human beings achieve their telos qua political animal and thus enjoy the good life. Other communities may not have the character of a moral community as long as participation in them is not considered a substantive good both *for* and *by* its members but rather a merely extrinsic or instrumental good (one might think here of purely economic communities held together only by self-interest). If the state is this latter sort of community, however, the concept of political friendship has little meaningful role to play.

Political friendship, then, is the bond that holds members of the political community (i.e., citizens) in ties of mutual solidarity qua citizens. That is, members of the political community encounter one another, first, as free and equal (and hence not as masters and servants, but potentially as friends), and second, as fellow participants in a set of shared goods or a project valued by both as a common good.[1] All friendships are mediated by some vision of the good, and correspondingly all communities formed in accordance with a shared vision of the good display a form of friendship. If the state can be thought of as a moral community, then its members are friends in a particular sense. This implies, I should point out, not only viewing *political communities in general* as shared goods, but also so viewing the *particular community* of which one is a member; one is not the political friend of all persons living in any state (even in any just state), but of those participating in one's own political community. Political friendship thus implies a certain degree of "patriotism": common commitment to participation in one's own political community as a common good, and hence to one's fellow citizens as integral parts of that good (after all, one views one's friend as a good and desires that friend's good).

The view of the state as a moral community held together by a political friendship stands opposed to both proceduralist and agonistic views of justice and participation in the political community. Proceduralist views see the just functioning of the state as the consistent and fair application of principles for the adjudication of disputes between autonomous persons or between communities, rather than the achievement of some *substantive good* or end of the community as a whole. Citizen participation in a proceduralist polity requires willingness to abide by the principles of justice (usually determined in terms of positive rights and duties), but no substantive commitment to the common good beyond a willingness to distribute these rights equally and consistently.[2]

Agonistic views, on the other hand, see the aim of political participation to be the establishment of one's own (or one's own community's) view of the good as the ruling principle of state action and policy. However, this view

1. Thus not merely as private goods (i.e., good for me), nor even as what Charles Taylor calls "convergent" goods (goods that, though achieved by collective actions, are still only private goods, not in principle shared). Cf. Taylor 1995: 190. Friendship is by definition a shared, rather than convergent, good, and, correspondingly, political friendship means viewing common participation in the state (which is constitutive of this relation) as a common good.

2. Rawls's conception of "public reason" is perhaps paradigmatic here.

is in principle opposed to that of other members in the political community (if it can be so called), and hence it involves struggle and opposition of interests, values, and principles rather than shared commitment to some vision of the common good. In agonistic polities, the only bond holding together citizens is their common commitment to using the machinery of state (elections, the courts, etc.) to advance their conception of the good. This is a far cry from the substantive commitment that founds political friendships. Since both proceduralism and agonism view participation in the state to be instrumental to either merely private or convergent goods, in the eyes of one committed to the ideal of political friendship, they both yield a conception of the political community that makes being asked to sacrifice or die for one's polis about as compelling as being asked to die for the phone company or for a god one does not believe in.[3]

Obviously this ideal places a strong emphasis on common commitments rather than convergent private interests, and this has led certain partisans of the ideal of political friendship to strongly oppose participation by citizens in other moral communities that could divide their interests from the common good and thus divide their commitment to the political community. Rousseau is perhaps the best example here. He opposes the creation of any "sectional associations" within a republic in the name of protecting the general will from degeneration into private wills (Rousseau 1968: book 2, chapter 3). In other words, for Rousseau, not only should the state *be* a moral community for its members, but it should be their *primary,* even *only,* moral community.

Such views, of course, are extremely bothersome to associational pluralists like Kuyper, and this can lead to generalized suspicion of the concepts of political friendship and of the state as a moral community.[4] However, these concepts need not necessarily lead to a kind of statism or undifferentiated collectivism, as evidenced by Aristotle's articulation of it. For the Philosopher, too much unity in a state is a direct threat to the possibility of political friendship, since friendship can only be between free and equal — and hence, different, integral — persons or communities.[5] Furthermore, though the political community is for him the end or perfection of all pre-

3. The remark about the phone company comes from Alasdair MacIntyre; see Horton and Mendus 1994: 303.

4. For Kuyper, the degree to which the Rousseauian version of this ideal played a role in inspiring the French Revolution just compounds the concern. Of course, just what this degree is, is a topic of much scholarly debate.

5. Cf. *Nicomachean Ethics* 8.9-11, and *Politics* 2.2-5, in Aristotle 1984.

political communities, it does not for that reason extinguish them. Families, villages, and other communities are subordinated to the political community as lower ends to their perfection, but that does not extinguish their particularity or a certain degree of integrity and autonomy on their part. Within Aristotle's political community, other communities flourish. What prevents this from threatening the commitment to the common good constitutive of political friendship is the fact that these communities are *subsidiary* to the state, which is considered as a community of communities. Commitment to the good of one's family is compatible with commitment to the common good of the political community since the former community is a subsidiary part of the latter. Thus a certain kind of associational plurality can be preserved, even in light of the ideal of political friendship.[6] We will see, however, that, in articulating a Kuyperian version of the ideal, this Aristotelian defense of associational pluralism will not do, since Kuyper rejects the notion of a subsidiary relationship between nonpolitical spheres and the state.

II. The Necessity of Political Friendship for Democracy

I want to argue now that the ideal of political friendship (with the concomitant view of the state as a moral community) is a necessary part of a workable understanding of the conditions that make democracies possible. Without a sense of participating with one's fellow citizens in a common good, the impetus for genuine democratic action in the political is lost. Without some realization of this ideal, democratic polities degenerate into (merely) procedural or agonistic republics, neither of which is sustainably democratic.

Charles Taylor makes an argument to this effect in his discussion of the liberal/communitarian debate. Central, he argues, to the civic humanist tradition is a conception of freedom whereby a society is only free where its citizens can have "a sense that the political institutions in which they live are an expression of themselves" (Taylor 1995: 187). When citizens can identify with the state and its laws as a result of their active participation in it, they are not *subjects* to external forces but enjoy their full *dignity as citizens* and are therefore free; we can call this a "participatory" definition of freedom. If political participation — and the resultant identification with the laws — is constitutive of political freedom, civic virtue is a necessary component of freedom; a

---

6. Cf. Aristotle, *Politics* 1, in Aristotle 1984.

free polity is one in which citizens are ready to put their private interests to the side and engage publicly in the interests of the common good.

Without this disposition on the part of citizens, each could identify only with laws that advanced or protected his or her private good and hence this identification would in no sense be a reflection of each's dignity qua citizen. Civic virtue constitutes a form of patriotism that binds citizens together in common commitment to participation in a shared project: "the bond of solidarity with my compatriots in a functioning republic is based on a sense of shared fate, where the sharing itself is of value" (192). Each citizen is bound with others in the project of realizing a polity that reflects their dignity as citizens, that is, a polity that is *free* in the participatory sense. This is a bond that one shares with other members of one's own polity in a way that it is not shared with members of other polities; it cannot be reduced to cosmopolitan commitment to the dignity and welfare of all persons, since it concerns *citizen* dignity expressed in a *particular* constitution and set of laws. In other words, a participatory concept of freedom and the dignity of citizens entails a conception of the polis as a moral community and of a political friendship with one's fellow citizens.

Taylor then goes on to argue that political friendship — understood in terms of a patriotism of civic virtue — plays a crucial role in maintaining liberal democratic regimes. It is necessary, he says, for citizens of democratic societies to respond with outrage to "violations of the norms of liberal self-rule" (195) — amongst which he cites the Iran-contra affair and Watergate. This kind of outrage cannot be sustained by an atomistic citizenry estranged from a shared commitment to the common good and lacking the ability to identify with the laws of the land as expressing their collective participation in this common good. In other words, only a sense that scandals like Watergate are an outrage against our *collective dignity as citizens of this political community* can sustain the kind of outrage necessary to sustain liberal democratic regimes. Neither self-interest nor an abstract, cosmopolitan commitment to "universal principle unalloyed with particular identifications" (197) can fund the degree and extent of the required sense of outrage. What made Americans unwilling to accept Watergate (or Canadians to accept the Sponsorship scandal) was not individual self-interest nor commitment to abstract principles of fair play, but a sense that their *collective dignity as American citizens* was violated by the contravention of the norms of democratic self-rule; it was their patriotism of civic virtue — and their sense that their political community at its best exemplifies and enshrines their dignity as citizens — that underlay their response. Thus, without some sense of the state as a moral community and one's citizens as one's political friends, the degree of commitment to the common good of one's particular political community necessary to resist violations of democratic norms cannot be generated or sustained.

If proceduralism, according to Taylor, is insufficient to maintain democracy, then agonism too endangers the beating heart of democratic polities. Jean Bethke Elshtain argues that two developments in modern politics are moving Western political life in decidedly undemocratic directions. In the "politics of displacement," people no longer engage one another in public discourse in accordance with their *public identity* as *citizens* but rather appear in public clothed entirely in their various *private identities* (gender, race, sexual orientation), and hence public discourse degenerates into struggles for full recognition of private differences rather than being animated by shared orientation toward the achievement of some genuinely *public* good (cf. Elshtain 1995: chapter 2). These politics, then, become a "politics of difference" wherein the kind of community with which citizens identify is the "we" of homogenous private identity groups (the "gay community," "the Quebecois" community) rather than the "we" of a variegated citizenry engaged *together* in a project of deliberation, argumentation, and compromise aimed at the good of the community as a whole (chapter 3). The recognition of difference is indeed crucial to pluralistic democracies, but, when confronted with someone with a different private identity, "my recognition of her difference, by which I mean my preparedness to engage her as an interlocutor *given* our differences on the things that count politically . . . turns on the fact that I share something with her. She is in the world with me; she, too, is *a citizen*" (67). Recognition of difference is necessary to treating others in accordance with their dignity, but in political matters, this means also recognizing their dignity qua citizens.

Without this recognition of a shared public identity, political discourse degenerates into "incommensurability" — the inability to actually understand and engage one another on a level playing field — and hence into zero-sum struggles for recognition rather than genuinely democratic deliberation, argumentation, and compromise. Democratic politics for Elshtain — as for Taylor — requires commitment to the political community as a shared good and to its members as political friends (i.e., citizens). As with Aristotle, this by no means implies that democratic political communities must be either institutionally or directionally homogenous; rather that political friendship is a condition that makes democratic polities possible in associationally and culturally diverse societies.

III. Kuyperian Barriers to Political Friendship

Abraham Kuyper is committed to both democratic governance and the "multiformity" of society, both structurally (i.e., to the plurality of different types of institutions and associations within society) and directionally (i.e., to the plurality of different "world-and-life views" within a political community).[7] If Taylor and Elshtain are correct (and we will assume for present purposes that they are), then it is crucial that his political vision include some account of (or at least the possibility of) (1) the state as a moral community; (2) the capacity of members of that community to recognize one another as "political friends" (i.e., as participants in a shared project constituting a genuinely common good); and (3) the grounds for a patriotism of civic virtue focused on this particular political community rather than on a cosmopolitan view of abstract political right. Kuyper's means of explicating two of his central commitments seem to put up barriers to such an account.

In the first case, the associational pluralism for which Kuyper is rightly praised makes it difficult to see how it is possible for him to articulate a sense of the state as a moral community. As we've seen in the case of both Aristotle and Elshtain, commitment to a flourishing associational life outside of (or at least not identical with) the sphere of the state is not necessarily a barrier to civic friendship (Rousseau notwithstanding). However, Kuyper's "sphere sovereignty" account of the relation of civil society and the state undermines at least Aristotle's grounds[8] for the reconciliation of associational pluralism and civic friendship. In Aristotle's view, a logic of whole and parts defines the relation between the state and civil society: subsidiary moral communities have a degree of integrity and autonomy with respect to one another and the state, but only insofar as parts cannot be reduced to other parts nor assimilated wholesale into the whole.[9] As parts, the ends (and hence the moral

---

7. This distinction between types of pluralism comes from Mouw and Griffioen 1993.

8. Elshtain's account of this in "Democracy on Trial" is too focused on the attitudes and dispositions of citizens to elaborate a "political theoretical" account of this reconciliation in terms of a normative theory of the relation between the state and civil society.

9. One might use the image of a body. The hand has an integrity of its own, qua hand, and is hence autonomous from other parts of the body, and even has a degree of autonomy from the body as a whole in respect of its distinctive functions (only it can grasp, point, etc., and hence it performs these functions with a measure of autonomy). But these functions are only fully intelligible in light of the (subsidiary) role that their ends play with respect to the ends of the body as a whole (e.g., grasping an apple is only fully intelligible as a subsidiary part of the more general end of eating or sustaining the body).

character) of these communities are only made fully complete and intelligible as subsidiary ends to the telos of the political community (i.e., the good life as the life of active virtue). In other words, the moral character of civil society is derivative of the moral character of the political community (the state), on the Philosopher's telling.

For Kuyper, civil society is not subsidiary to the state and, correspondingly, the state is not the perfection or telos of the communities that constitute civil society. Though he occasionally refers to the state as "the sphere of spheres which encircles the whole extent of human life" (Kuyper 1998d: 472), this means only that, both within and between all spheres of human life, the state has a regulative role to play in securing justice. Justice, then, as the end of the state (and hence constitutive of its moral character), is universal in human life, but the ends of the various spheres of civil society do not derive from nor are subsidiary parts of justice conceived of as the ultimate end of human life. On the contrary, the moral characters of the spheres of civil society — their particular normative tasks — are a result of a direct mandate from God mediated (if at all) only by the order of creation, rather than by the authority of the state: "the family, the business, science, art and so forth are all social spheres, which do not owe their existence to the state, and which do not derive the law of their life from the superiority of the state, but obey a high authority within their own bosom; an authority which rules, by the grace of God, just as the sovereignty of the state does" (Kuyper 1961: 90). This being the case, it does not follow from moral commitment to an institution of civil society that one has a moral commitment to the political community; religious, scientific, recreational friendship does not logically entail political friendship. Thus Kuyper does not have open to him Aristotle's mode of reconciling associational pluralism and political friendship.

Furthermore, Kuyper's way of articulating the state/(civil) society distinction further complicates the possibility of committed participants in other moral communities also feeling a sense of commitment to the state as a moral community. Society — which encompasses all the spheres of civil society — is for Kuyper an *organic* phenomenon; unfolding in its multiform richness according to fundamental creational commands to human beings to develop their various potentials in service to and praise of their Creator. The bonds that hold the communities defined by the various sovereign spheres together are spontaneous, communal responses to a creational cultural mandate: in each sphere the natural sociality of human beings is expressed in the development of communities and institutions dedicated to particular normative tasks (child rearing, the pursuit of truth, the worship of God, etc.) (cf. Kuyper 1998d: 467; Kuyper 1961: 91-92). No deliberate intervention or construction on the part of human beings or institutions is needed for the unfolding and growth of these communities — only a willingness to respond faithfully to God's commandments. Thus the character of the spheres of society as *moral communities* (i.e., as authentic responses to a normative call from God) is articulated by Kuyper in terms of their *organic* character.

By contrast, the state has a *mechanical* character. For Kuyper, the only properly organic state would be "one organic world empire with God as its King" that served to unite the various families "in a higher unity" that "would have internally been bound up in the Kingship of God, which would have ruled regularly, directly and harmoniously in the hearts of all men" (Kuyper 1961: 92). Thus, if human beings had not fallen, there would have been no distinguishable political communities operating under human governance and in accordance with positive laws. Human governance and the existence of such states are a remedy for the effects of sin, not an authentic communal response to creational ordinances (and hence is not organic). Though divinely instituted, human political governance is "a *mechanical* head, which from without has been placed upon the trunk of the nation" (92-93).

The state has a normative call — to do justice — but this is fundamentally different in kind from that of the organic spheres of society. First, as just mentioned, this command is not a creational ordinance for human flourishing and the praise of God, but rather a mechanical remedy for the effects of sin on the healthy organic functioning of society. Second, the unifying force of the state is not natural human sociability but the power of the sword; that is, what holds a political community together and gives reality to its normative task is the power of coercion, rather than spontaneous communal response to differentiated creational ordinance.[10] The normative task of political governance (justice) is:

1. Whenever different spheres clash, to compel mutual regard for the boundary-lines of each; 2. To defend individuals and the weak ones in those spheres against the abuse of power of the rest; and 3. To coerce all

10. Thus the principal characteristic of government is the power of life and death. As will be discussed below, these different unifying principles make for inevitable tension between state power and organic civil society that must then be resisted by constitutional principles grounded in citizen participation in accordance with the mandate to resist state sovereignty.

together to bear *personal* and *financial* burdens for the maintenance of the natural unity of the state. (97)[11]

These tasks have the character of procedural principles for the regulation of boundary disputes between communities, on the one hand, and of the relations between individuals, on the other hand. They are not aimed — as are the creational commands founding the spheres of society — at the achievement of an intrinsic, substantive good, but merely at the prevention of harm for the sake of individuals and communities. In other words: in contrast to organic communities, the mechanical community of the state does not in itself constitute and provide a substantive common (and hence, shared) good for its citizens as a community, but merely a set of procedural principles and negative freedoms that constitute a convergent good for the individuals and communities of society. Thus, on the face of it at least, Kuyper's way of articulating the state/society distinction in terms of the mechanical/organic distinction makes it impossible to view the state itself as a moral community.

Furthermore, this view of the normative task of the state does not by definition imply the necessity of active citizen involvement in politics in pursuit of the common good. Civic virtue is expressed instead as a disposition on the part of members of society to *resist* the colonizing pressure of the state (cf. Kuyper 1998d: 473), rather than active involvement in the political community as such. Citizen participation in the making of laws is, on this view, a *prudential* consideration — owing to the greater likelihood of a democratic government protecting the rights and freedoms of members of society (cf. Kuyper 1961: 97-98) — rather than an *intrinsic* and necessary expression of the dignity of citizens. The dignity of human beings, on the contrary, is constituted by the *organic character of society,* not by participation in the state (given its mechanical character).[12]

Taylor, as we have seen, sees concern for the dignity of citizens — as ex-

11. "The natural unity of the state" — given what has just been said — cannot mean "its character as an organic community" but must simply refer to the unity necessary to perform its (mechanical and remedial) functions. Cf. also Kuyper 1998d: 472: "The various spheres of life cannot do without the State sphere, for just as one space can limit another, so one sphere can limit another unless the State fixes their boundaries by law."

12. "And finally to touch on the real point that lies at the heart of the social problem, the Christian religion *seeks personal human dignity* in the social relationships of an *organically integrated society.* The French revolution disturbed that organic tissue, broke those social bonds, and left nothing but the monotonous, self-seeking individual asserting his own self-sufficiency" (Kuyper 1991: 44, emphasis added).

pressed through their ability to identify with laws they have themselves participated in constructing — as essential for motivating resistance to antidemocratic movements. Similarly, Elshtain argues that recognition of others *as citizens* (i.e., as members of the political community) is necessary for genuinely democratic deliberation in a pluralistic society. In both cases, the capacity to treat *citizenship* as a substantive moral status — and one indissolubly connected with participation in political communities — is seen as an essential component of democracy. Kuyper's "mechanical" conception of the state makes this appear difficult to achieve (though as we'll see, other elements in his thought correspond closely with Taylor's and Elshtain's views).

The second of Kuyper's fundamental commitments that seems to sow difficulties for articulating a version of civic friendship is his commitment to *directional* (or "worldview") pluralism, particularly as this commitment intersects with his associational pluralism. Calvinism, Catholicism, socialism, liberalism, etc., all constitute "world-and-life views" or "life-systems" *(Weltanschauungen)*, each of which is understood as a deductive consequence of one fundamental principle (in Calvinism, this principle is the sovereignty of God). To those shaped by one or another of these systems, every aspect of life — and hence also their participation in various social spheres — is shaped by their commitment to its principles. There is no aspect or part of life, whether individual or communal, that is not shaped by one's life-system (hence the name).

Socially, this plurality of worldviews is expressed in the development of confessionally oriented institutions within civil society. Thus Calvinists have their churches, Catholics their own, communists their workers committees, and so on. But this is not the end of it. Even institutions that are "common" — that is, ones that do not by their nature or function represent one worldview community rather than another — are shaped by directional pluralism. Within the school, for example, the curriculum cannot be strictly neutral between, say, socialism and Calvinism; one or the other life-system must shape the curriculum and hence shape the minds and hearts of the students. Because of this, Kuyper often supported the development of parallel institutions, each performing the same function (e.g., schooling children, advocating for workers) but each shaped by a different world-and-life view; most famously for Kuyper the establishment of Christian educational institutions from day schools to the Vrije Universiteit, but also separate media and press networks, separate labor unions, etc.[13]

13. It is debatable to what extent Kuyper was committed to this kind of "pillarization"

This strategy for institutionalizing incompatible (and hence, competing) views of life in separate but parallel social institutions can in theory be extended to all social spheres but not to the state itself. At the level of politics, the various communities shaped by diverging world-and-life views must come together and participate in some form of shared practice. However, there is no neutral ground in politics either, and simple logic prevents these communities from abandoning their particular life-systems in the political sphere: "Even the most radical unbeliever, if he is a logical thinker, will have to grant that it is utterly absurd for a person to take such a confession of Christ on his lips and ignore the consequences that flow directly from it for our national politics" (Kuyper 1998c: 210). This means that political life too will be a locus of *principal struggle* between incompatible life-systems. For Kuyper this means that the various political options must be viewed ultimately in spiritual terms: "What we take exception to and resist is solely their disastrous *principle,* which is detached from Christ and which is the same in all these groups. Together [Liberals, Conservatives, Radicals, and Socialists] form a single spiritual family, bred from a single stock" (213). In spiritual struggles, though there may be temporary alliances, there can be no compromise: "But now we know that in our country too all spiritual conflict must finally culminate in being *for* or *against* Christ" (214).[14] Even between Calvinists and Catholics, though they both confess Christ, there can be only cooperation, never unity (cf. Kuyper 1998c: 218-19).

It would seem, then, that politics must ultimately be, for Kuyper, agonistic: a struggle between incompatible principles in a winner-take-all battle. All alliances can then only be strategic, temporary, and in principle tentative since no synthesis or unity is possible between antithetical spiritual principles. If this is the whole story, it is difficult to see how Kuyper could account for a set of fulsomely *shared* political values and goods that unite all citizens in a common commitment to and participation in a genuine political community. It would seem that Kuyper's politics is an incarnation of Elshtain's politics of displacement, wherein our public identities (as citizens) are reduced to (or replaced by) private identities (our religious or worldview

---

in all spheres of society as an integral part of his own worldview. Thus it is not absolutely clear that he consciously supported the full-scale pillarization of Dutch society. Nevertheless, many of his ideas and causes lead in this direction.

14. Kuyper goes so far as to say of those who seceded from the Antirevolutionary Party: "Really, they do not understand how by giving their vote to a Liberal in the context of our national struggle they are actually voting against their Lord" (Kuyper 1998c: 218). Cf. also Kuyper 1998d: 484.

identities) and thus we are able only to identify with the "we" constituted by our incompatible worldviews rather than a genuine political community.

IV. Kuyperian Resources for Political Friendship

It is close enough to a cliché to be true that Kuyper seeks to steer between the Scylla of liberal individualism and the Charybdis of collectivism, and that he does so in his championing of the central role of civil society in his doctrine of sphere sovereignty. If what I have said thus far is correct, he must also steer between proceduralism on the one hand and agonism on the other, with respect to his understanding of specifically political life. The fact that two central dimensions of his thought seem to pull him in opposite directions — his associational pluralism toward proceduralism and his directional pluralism toward agonism — actually suggests to me that he has resources aplenty to do so. In seeing how this is possible, I will disclose the resources in Kuyper's thought that point toward a Kuyperian conception of civic friendship (and hence of the state as a moral community).

In doing so, I want first to briefly establish that Kuyper has a sense of democratic politics that shares a number of important themes with the "civic humanist" tradition that Taylor articulates. First, Kuyper is a republican, at least of a certain sort. More than once he approvingly cites Calvin's (alleged) preference for republican forms of governance, on the grounds that "it is safer and better to let several people together steer the ship of state so that one may restrain the other when the lust for power might degenerate into tyranny" (John Calvin, cited in Kuyper 1998a: 285).[15] Citizen government of the republican kind is the most effective in discharging the normative task of the state, given the corruptive power of human sin. In fact, a sense of sin is, for Kuyper, constitutive of the impetus that establishes and maintains constitutional governments in which the liberties of citizens (including their liberty to participate in government) are protected. It grounds "a just constitution that restrains abuses of authority, sets limits, and offers the people a natural protection against lust for power and arbitrariness" (310). In other words, for Kuyper, a republican government is best at ensuring the *negative freedoms* of its subjects and their communities from intru-

---

15. Cf. also Kuyper 1961: 83. Heslam suggests that this attribution of republicanism to Calvin may be disingenuous, but since our concern here is Kuyper's views, it can here go unchallenged. Cf. Heslam 1998.

sion and abuse by either the state, individuals, or other social spheres; this is very much in keeping with the previous discussion of the "mechanical" character of the state.

But there is an element of Kuyper's "republicanism" that goes beyond, and (perhaps) exists in tension with, his sense of the mechanical character of government. Beyond merely being best at securing the *negative liberties* of those subject to a government, a republican form of government embodies the *positive freedoms* of *citizens*. Genuine political freedom is not "the free rein for arbitrariness" but rather "ours is a genuine *civil, and also moral freedom that does not disrupt but unites,* that derives its support precisely from *legitimate authority,* that offers and guarantees justice so that we may without fear consecrate heart, head and hand to what is good and beautiful, noble and just" (281, quoting John Winthrop). This freedom is inseparable from active political participation by citizens, without which (negative) liberty would merely divide and authority would be illegitimate. Kuyper cites Alexis de Tocqueville in defense of the notion that active, cooperative participation of citizens in government is necessary for the maintenance of genuine liberty: "Nonetheless, the sharp criticism by the liberal de Tocqueville remains justified: 'These citizens, who appear to be so interested in their freedom, year upon year relinquish almost unnoticeably part of their individual independence to the administrative arm. The very people who have brought down thrones and put the kings of the earth beneath their feet bow before the whims of an ordinary civil servant without any protest'" (281, quoting Tocqueville).

This *laissez aller* attitude is an abrogation of "the noble civic spirit" and of the proper pride of citizens in their status as citizens; in other words, it is a crisis of *civic virtue* and a sense of the *dignity* of citizenship. Where this civic virtue is in decline, the necessary checks on the power and extent of the state are removed and the way is paved for a rollback of even the negative freedoms of individuals and the spheres of society: "Freedom is in danger precisely when citizens lack pride and the state lacks bounds" (283).[16] Thus the positive liberties of *citizens* — the freedom to participate in government in accordance with their dignity qua citizens — make possible and preserve their negative freedoms *as individuals and members of society.*

This view of Kuyper's is grounded not just in a concern to mitigate the effects of sin, but in his positive Calvinistic vision of human flourishing and

---

16. For a similar account of the role of civic virtue in maintaining negative freedoms, see Kuyper 1998d: 473.

the proper role and nature of government. Constitutional governments alone, he argues, can create the framework within which the various spheres of society can develop organically and thus flourish in accordance with God's creational commands for them, since they alone secure the proper boundaries of the various spheres and of the state itself (see Kuyper 1998a). Furthermore, in "Maranatha" Kuyper argues that "popular influence" is "inherent in the nature of a constitutional government" to such an extent that it "cannot rest until it has touched bottom" (Kuyper 1998c: 223). In other words, the very logic of legitimate constitutional governments requires the fullest extent of popular influence, even to the extent of the enfranchisement of the "little people." Citizen government (republicanism) is not merely a prudential preference for Kuyper based on its greater likelihood of success in minimizing corruption and injustice in government, but a *positive require-ment* grounded in what he takes to be the fundamental commitment of Calvinism to the flourishing of society and the belief, in turn, that this requires constitutional government.[17]

Thus Kuyper's republicanism includes an account of what Taylor characterizes as "a participatory concept of freedom," one in which freedom is not separated from a palpable sense of and concern for the *dignity of citizens*. But, as we've seen, implicit in this commitment is a sense of the political community as a moral community and of one's fellow citizens as "political friends" (i.e., fellow participants in the political community, viewed by each as a shared good). If my discussion above is correct, this stands in tension with Kuyper's view of the state as a merely "mechanical" institution, the good of which is constituted merely by its role in restraining the social effects of sin. Such a view explains only the importance of the protections of politically negative freedoms (i.e., the freedoms of members of society and civil society from intrusion by others). But since Kuyper himself seems to ground the possibility of these negative freedoms on an account of the politically positive freedoms of citizens, he seems himself to transcend the limits of a merely mechanical conception of the state.

So the question then arises: What are the possibilities of articulating a Kuyperian conception of the state as a moral community, and hence a conception that can support a commitment to the centrality of positive political freedoms grounded in a robust conception of citizen dignity? What would a

---

17. "Indeed, has not the entire Calvinist movement — in Great Britain, the Netherlands, and America alike — relied precisely on *the extension of popular influence* to strengthen their governments?" (Kuyper 1998c: 223).

Kuyperian view of citizen dignity and civic virtue (inextricably interlinked concepts) look like? My account of this will have two stages. First I will briefly discuss the doctrine of common grace as a way of overcoming the tendency of Kuyper's directional pluralism to slide into a kind of agonism. Then I will discuss the possibility of viewing the state as an "organic" social sphere in its own right and hence of viewing it as a moral community in a robust sense. This will then also deal with the Charybdis of proceduralism (which Kuyper's views about positive freedoms commit him to slaying — or at least avoiding).

As we have seen, the fact that Kuyper sees the antithesis as both *radical* and *ubiquitous* seems to condemn his view of participation in the public sphere to an agonism in line with Elshtain's worries about the anti-democratic character of the "politics of displacement." While never effacing both of these characteristics of the antithesis, Kuyper's conception of *common grace* serves to "soften the edges" of that doctrine, if you will. Through common grace, God restrains the effects of sin in human beings and in society, allowing a degree of genuine creational goodness to be expressed even in the actions, organizations, and commitments of the unregenerate. Furthermore, the realm of common grace (social institutions, etc., that are not based explicitly on Christian principles) can itself be shaped and "ennobled" through the influence of special grace: "It [the church] must purify and ennoble the ideas in general circulation, elevate public opinion, introduce more solid principles, and so raise the view of life prevailing in the state, society and the family" (Kuyper 1998b: 195).

Finally, just because Christians (and the church as an organic social expression) are recipients of special grace, this does not imply that they too are without need for or participation in common grace. Indeed, Christian social institutions are "the terrain of special grace that has utilized the data of common grace" (199) (including the results of scientific investigation, artistic creation, etc., in the realms of common grace). In both its restraint of sin and its mutual susceptibility with special grace to the positive influence of the other, common grace can thus offer some part of the groundwork for a more robust cooperation between Christians and non-Christians in the public sphere. Though ultimately the principal divide remains, Christians in the public sphere can unite with non-Christians in their affirmation of certain common goods, since common grace allows non-Christians to see what is good and true in Christian ideals, and vice versa. Thus understanding "citizenship" and the political community as an expression of common grace (particularly when under the influence of special grace) can provide grounds for viewing it as a shared good, in a way that agonism makes impossible.

However, common grace by itself is insufficient for the needed understanding of citizen dignity, the state as a moral community, and civic friendship. This is because — as discussed above — it cannot be a general or universal commitment to certain ("cosmopolitan") principles that anchors civic friendship, but a commitment to viewing *this or that particular state* as a moral community and thus a shared good (and correspondingly to viewing *one's fellow citizens* rather than "citizens in general" as one's political friends). Common grace is distributed universally, since it is primarily a grace that upholds the structures of creation, not one focused on this or that community, person, or activity. Hence it does not by itself underwrite a sense of political friendship, though it does provide some of the necessary groundwork.

What more is needed in order to be able to see one's own political community as a particular but shared good is also what is needed to defuse the temptation of proceduralism, namely, a vision of the political community as an authentic communal response to creational commands aimed at human flourishing (i.e., as an organism). This would allow this particular political community to be seen as a common project, aimed at the realization of a shared (at least to some extent) vision of human flourishing and thus of one's fellow citizens as equal participants in this project simply in virtue of being in community, rather than in virtue of a particular set of religious or ideological commitments. Though this requires rejecting Kuyper's view of politics and government as merely mechanical, it is in keeping with other significant aspects of his thought.

I want to get at this possibility by examining what it might mean to talk about the state as a "sphere" of society. Kuyper occasionally uses this term in association with the state, but his view of its mechanical character prevents him from fully exploring what is implied thereby. The idea of a social sphere indicates, I want to argue, *both* an organic community participating in the realization of an aspect of human flourishing *and* a set of institutional arrangements developed to organize and facilitate these organic, communal activities. Kuyper most clearly presents this view when he discusses the distinction and connection between "the church as institute" and "the church as organism": "*Institute* is related to *organism* as that which has been *built* to that which has *grown*. All that has been constructed of parts and pieces or *established* by force from without is an *institute*; an *organism*, on the other hand, is anything which its vital parts have produced on their own and which, subject to changes in its form, perpetuates and enlarges its own life" (187).

The church as an organism is the "mystical body of Christ existing partly in heaven, partly on earth," whereas the church as institute is "a local and temporally constructed *institution* grounded in human choices, decisions, and acts of the will" (187). Any concrete church — say, the Gereformeerde Kerken in Nederland or the Christian Reformed Church, or indeed any congregation where "two or three are gathered" — manifests both an institutional side and an organic side, the former giving concrete, local expression to the dynamic beating heart provided by the latter. It is not difficult to expand this characterization to all social spheres: all communities in civil society manifest both institutional particularity, organization, and administration, on the one hand, and organic community, development, and flourishing on the other. The school, for example, is both a community of educators and students working together in response to God's cultural mandate (organic side) and a set of institutions, policies, rules, and standards (institutional side). Both sides are necessary to count as what I have been calling a "moral community" — one in which members understand their participation in this particular community to be with others for a common good. The "organic" side provides the moral goodness that is communally shared (since it is a response to commands for human flourishing), and the "institutional" side provides the framework for distinguishing this community as a *particular* expression or pursuit of that moral good and hence as *one's own* community.

Now, Kuyper's view of the state as mechanical would seem to restrict it to having only an "institutional side" and hence prevent it from being a genuine social sphere and a moral community. Government, on this view, works through the "institutional" means of construction (the assembly of disparate pieces)[18] and establishment by force, rather than through the organic growth and development of a moral community. If this is so, then this further relegates citizen participation from the center of political action, in spite of Kuyper's insistence that constitutional government by its essence involves citizen participation (see above). However, if we reject this "one-sided" view of the political community, there is a genuine possibility for seeing the state also as an organic community, as long as we can find some kind of "political" organic correlate to the political institution of government

18. These are the various ideological communities within the state, on the one hand, and the social spheres, on the other — the former arrayed in opposing fundamental principles and the latter as responses to different creational commands and hence as having differing normative tasks. The state's job is to put something together out of this disparate (even opposed) array — a job of patchwork rather than "growth."

(construed as administration). With this organic side in place — a kind of "political public sphere" organized around a shared vision of the good — we have grounds for seeing the political sphere as a genuine community, even a moral community. But what, for Kuyper, could this be?

It is not sufficient, as already indicated, for the "public sphere" to be merely a set of forums for either agonistic struggle between publics or the exercise by individuals of merely procedural "public reason" (à la Rawls); there must be community around some substantive vision of a genuinely common good. I want to argue that, for Kuyper, this public sphere is (can be seen to be) constituted by the *nation* as the organic correlate to the institution of political governance. On the one hand, the (ethnic) nation is an organic community that is grown, rather than consciously assembled (at least in the case of, say, the Netherlands — the situation of postnational states will have to wait), since it develops in accordance with a shared history, language, cuisine, and — most importantly — a common "national character,"[19] all of which are not assemblages of disparate parts nor are imposed by force. All these aspects of nationhood can be conceived as particular expressions of human flourishing in accordance with creational commands (they put the "culture" in the cultural mandate, if you will). Every Dutch person is in organic community with every other Dutch person, then, regardless of divisions of class, ideology, gender, age, etc.[20]

But none of this yet constitutes a view of the nation as grounded in a shared vision of the good; in other words, as constituted (at least in part) by common values, commitments, projects, etc., rather than merely by shared habits, dispositions, and tastes. The capacity of a national political community to share a vision of the good, given the reality of the antithesis, depends upon the actual influence of special grace on the national psyche of the whole, in keeping with the general capacity of special grace to "ennoble" common grace; that is, only if it is a Christian nation, but one with which non-Christians can identify on account of the work of common grace. On the one side, the Christian citizen can share a vision of the good with her non-Christian countrymen if the national character and dispositions — which are manifestations of common grace — reflect a significant degree of the benign influence of special grace.

19. Kuyper uses this concept repeatedly, particularly when discussing the effects of Calvinism on English, Dutch, and American cultures in Kuyper 1998a.

20. "Our national society is, as Da Costa said, 'not a heap of souls on a piece of ground,' but rather a God-willed community, a living human organism" (Kuyper 1991: 52).

Thus, in "Maranatha" Kuyper enjoins his Antirevolutionary *mannen-broeders,* if they have "true patriotic love," to "rise to the defense of the honour of Christ in politics" out of hope that the "anti-Christian principle . . . has not yet scorched shut the conscience of this nation" (Kuyper 1998c: 214). Love of country is inseparable from love of Christ, since the Netherlands has a "national conscience" shaped by Calvinist principles that persists even in spite of the ascendancy of non-Christian principles in politics. Correspondingly, the non-Christian citizen shares values with his Christian countrymen since his own conscience is shaped in accordance with this national conscience that bears the mark of extensive Christian influence. Thus, in a Christian nation no one is a recipient of special grace in virtue of her nationality, but "public opinion, the general mind-set, the ruling ideas, the moral norms, the laws and customs there clearly betoken the influence of Christian faith. Though this is attributable to special grace, it is manifested on the terrain of common grace, i.e., in ordinary civil life" (Kuyper 1998b: 199). In a Christian nation, the national character and its moral intuitions are so shaped by Christian ideals that we can legitimately talk of a shared sense of the good transcending, but not neutral between, communities based on differing fundamental principles.

V. Conclusion: And Postnational States

Thus, by viewing the ethnic nation as the organic correlate of the government, there are grounds for viewing the national political community as a moral community and thus hope for viewing one's fellow citizens as fellow participants in a shared project organized around a shared vision of the common good. Kuyper's Netherlands, then, was a place where there was a real possibility of political friendship and hence of steering between the antidemocratic options of proceduralism and agonism. This possibility, of course, depends on a shared national history, culture, and sets of dispositions and habits. In other words, it works only for a genuine nation-state (and then, only one that is a "Christian nation"). This solution does not seem to guide those of us living in postnational states (North American states being paradigmatic, but the same seems to hold increasingly for European nations) that lack a sufficiently widespread sense of national community. I will conclude, then, with some (very) brief suggestions about how to apply what we've learned to these situations.

What is requisite universally for a sense of political friendship, in

Kuyper's terms, is the existence of an organic public sphere acting as the correlate to the "mechanical" institution of government. These two sides, furthermore, need to be intertwined to an extent that — in Taylor's terms now, but in accordance with Kuyper's republicanism — citizens can identify with the laws and acts of the state as their own qua citizens. One cannot hope to "assemble" a *national* identity where there is no shared history, since "assemblage" is an institutional means, and what is needed is organic "growth." But there is no necessity that the organic side of the state be any sort of nation, in the sense of possessing a shared history, language, culture, set of traditions, dispositions, or characteristics, only that the public sphere be shaped in accordance with the spontaneous community-building dispositions of citizens seeking a common good.

Perhaps we can employ Dooyeweerd's distinction between the internal and external functions of the state to guide us in thinking about this. In its "external" functions, the state regulates (aspects of) the enkaptic relations between other societal structures and also promotes justice for individuals within those social structures — very much in keeping with Kuyper's "mechanical" conception of the role of government. However, the state simultaneously has "internal functions" concerning relations "between government and citizens or between different branches of government."[21] Some of these functions are purely regulative, but there is ample space for viewing the norms for relations between government and citizens, and hence also between citizens as such, as being norms *for human flourishing* in a particular mode, and not simply as procedural dispute-resolution or border-regulation principles. No essential reference needs to be made here to a national character, etc., but only to a substantive, normed relationship aiming at a genuine *human good.*

The ideal of public justice, then, as the "name" for the totality of the state's normative task, includes both regulative principles (external functions) *and* substantive goods; the difference being marked by whether the norms at stake are aimed at the internal or the enkaptic/external functions of the sphere in question. Thus agonism is avoided by relying on shared norms for the internal functioning of the state — including the relations between citizens qua citizens (political relationships between individuals) — and proceduralism is avoided by showing that at least some norms for political activity are more than regulative, but are substantial directives for human flourishing. "Political friendship" here can be understood — in Dooye-

---

21. For a helpful discussion, see Chaplin 2007: 131.

weerd's technical vocabulary — as the ethical anticipation in juridical functioning, particularly in its internal functions.

References

Aristotle. 1984. *The Complete Works of Aristotle: The Revised Oxford Translation.* Edited by J. Barnes. Princeton: Princeton University Press.

Bratt, James D., ed. 1998. *Abraham Kuyper: A Centennial Reader.* Grand Rapids: Eerdmans.

Chaplin, J. 2007. "Public Justice as a Critical Political Norm." *Philosophia Reformata* 72, no. 2, pp. 130-50.

Elshtain, J. B. 1995. *Democracy on Trial.* Boston: Basic Books.

Heslam, P. S. 1998. *Creating a Christian Worldview: Abraham Kuyper's Lectures on Calvinism.* Grand Rapids: Eerdmans.

Horton, J., and S. Mendus. 1994. *After MacIntyre: Critical Perspectives on the Work of Alasdair MacIntyre.* Notre Dame, Ind.: University of Notre Dame Press.

Kuyper, Abraham. 1961. *Lectures on Calvinism.* Grand Rapids: Eerdmans.

———. 1991. *The Problem of Poverty.* Edited by J. Skillen. Grand Rapids: Baker.

———. 1998a. "Calvinism: The Source and Stronghold of Our Constitutional Liberties." Translated by R. Bruinsma. In *Abraham Kuyper: A Centennial Reader,* edited by James D. Bratt, pp. 279-322. Grand Rapids: Eerdmans.

———. 1998b. "Common Grace." Translated by J. Vriend. In *Abraham Kuyper: A Centennial Reader,* edited by James D. Bratt, pp. 165-201. Grand Rapids: Eerdmans.

———. 1998c. "Maranatha." Translated by J. Vriend. In *Abraham Kuyper: A Centennial Reader,* edited by James D. Bratt, pp. 205-29. Grand Rapids: Eerdmans.

———. 1998d. "Sphere Sovereignty." Translated by G. Kamp. In *Abraham Kuyper: A Centennial Reader,* edited by James D. Bratt, pp. 461-90. Grand Rapids: Eerdmans.

Mouw, R., and S. Griffioen. 1993. *Pluralisms and Horizons.* Grand Rapids: Eerdmans.

Rousseau, J. J. 1968. *The Social Contract.* Translated by Maurice Cranston. Harmondsworth: Penguin.

Taylor, C. 1995. "Cross Purposes: The Liberal-Communitarian Debate." In *Philosophical Argument.* Cambridge: Harvard University Press.

Covenant Theology for a Secular Society: Abraham Kuyper's *De Leer der Verbonden* (1880) as an Experiment in Modern Theology

John Halsey Wood, Jr.

Confessional theologians in the nineteenth century were usually supporters of conservative society. In the case of Abraham Kuyper, however, things were different. Kuyper was indeed a confessional theologian by any standard, but he was not an unwavering defender of traditional society. Orthodoxy in Kuyper's hands often turned out to be quite untraditional. How could confessional Calvinism be brought into rapport with modern society, and what did this mean for life within and outside of the church? These were Kuyper's central concerns.

The experiment involved here is twofold. First, several theologians have compared Kuyper's covenant theology to that of his forerunners in the Reformed tradition. Kuyper's theology, however, needs to be set in its own historical and social context in order to fully understand not only what Kuyper was saying but also what he was doing through his theology. Owen Chadwick's warning is timely: "[We] do not fathom intellectual history if they ask about nothing but the intellect" (Chadwick 1975: 13). This article is an experiment to that end. It begins, therefore, with a brief description of Kuyper's social context. In this context, *The Doctrine of the Covenant* (*De Leer der Verbonden*, 1909) shows itself as Kuyper's own experiment in bringing covenant theology into rapport with the times. Though he repeated this experiment later with different results, this article limits itself to the 1880 treatise.

This experiment was especially in service of the church, which in the nineteenth century was embattled on several fronts. Kuyper began these articles on the doctrine of the covenant in the fall of 1880, the same fall that the Free University of Amsterdam opened its doors. Kuyper's covenant theology supported the vision of a modern, differentiated society that he laid out in his inaugural lecture for the Free University, "Sphere Sovereignty." Specifically, covenant theology provided part of the theological rationale for the church as a modern institution in two ways. Covenant demonstrated the sovereignty and legitimacy of the church as a separate social institution by defining its boundaries. Second, by explaining the church's divine origin and task in covenantal terms, Kuyper responded to the modernist theologians who thought the church had become obsolete in modern society.

I. "Secularization"

The questions revolving around what happened to religion in the modern West are far from resolved. Generally, it seems that the reports of the death of God "have been greatly exaggerated." Nonetheless, if carefully defined, secularization is a useful category. "Secularization" refers to a variety of social processes, but two are especially in view here. First, secularization refers primarily to the social and historical process of institutional and functional differentiation — the separation of church and state, in short, and all its concomitants. Not included here, however, is the *inevitable* decline and privatization of religion. Referring to the classical notion of secularization in which the decline thesis was central, José Casanova explains: "The main fallacy in the [traditional] theory of secularization . . . is the confusion of historical processes of secularization proper [i.e., institutional and functional differentiation] with the alleged and anticipated consequences which those processes were supposed to have upon religion" (Casanova 1994: 19). John Sommerville concurs, and he points out that in certain situations "we can quite properly speak of a secular society which contains an entirely religious population" (Sommerville 1998: 251). Something like that was the experience of the Netherlands toward the close of the nineteenth century. In addition, Sommerville and others also observe intellectual parallels to the societal aspect of secularization. With regard to mentalities, Sommerville describes secularization as the shift of interest from ultimate to more proximate concerns.

Finally, it is useful to recognize the competitive and pluralizing nature of secularization especially with regard to the Dutch situation. In his study of European secularization, Hugh McLeod argues that pluralization is the "key" to the religious situation in late-nineteenth-century Europe. He concludes, "Rather than seeing secularization as an impersonal 'process' . . . it would be better to see it as a 'contest,' in which adherents of rival world-views battled it out" (McLeod 2000: 28). The proliferation of distinct worldviews was part of Kuyper's context, and he was a key participant in this process.

Recognition of the different aspects and the dynamism of secularization is important for understanding Kuyper and the Dutch situation. In particular, it allows one to accept otherwise apparently contradictory trends such as emboldened confessionalism and societal secularization (the narrowing sphere of religious institutions). These were both present in nineteenth-century Netherlands and even promoted by Kuyper himself.

II. Secularization Dutch Style

Some have suggested that secularization in the Netherlands did not occur until after World War II. This supposition is often based on the idea that secularization meant inevitable decline in religious practice. Yet, given the above revised characterization of secularization, it is clear that secularization was occurring already in the nineteenth century.

Specifically, institutional differentiation was occurring, and Abraham Kuyper was a key agent. Kuyper's passion since his student days at Leiden University had been the "church question." His vision, in contrast to the Dutch *volkskerk,* was a free church, a church loosed from the chains of the state and composed of freely consenting believers. A related concern was education. Kuyper wanted schools that would not be dominated by centralized governmental control but in which education could proceed freely according to the dictates of conscience. These two concerns came together practically and theoretically in the founding of the Free University of Amsterdam and Kuyper's inaugural lecture, "Sphere Sovereignty." "Sphere Sovereignty" was a plan for a differentiated, that is, secularized, society in which institutions such as the church and school could operate according to their own laws of life.

Kuyper pursued not just a church separated from the state, but also a church separated from the university. Kuyper realized this vision with the establishment of the Free University of Amsterdam in 1880. Several years prior, the 1876 education law had raised the question of the spheres of church, state, and academy. This law created the *duplex ordo* system in the theological faculties of the *rijksuniversiteit.* Under this system the church retained its right to appoint professors of theology but the state now made appointments for disciplines such as biblical studies, which followed the "scientific" method. In 1880 Kuyper published several articles describing his own view of the relation between the theological faculty and the church. Kuyper's proposal was, from the perspective of institutional differentiation, an even more radically secularizing one than the 1876 law, for he granted the church no right at all to appoint members of the theological faculty of the university. Of course, Kuyper held that the university should not name professors who were not Reformed and professors remained accountable to the church for their views, but the relationship between the two institutions was essentially voluntary (see Kuyper 1880a and Kuyper 1890).

Another law in 1878 established the religious neutrality of the public schools. This time, however, Kuyper rejected this kind of intellectual secularization, because it privileged so-called "neutral" worldviews over religious ones. Religious neutrality was a myth, said Kuyper. This position was complex. Kuyper insisted on institutional separation but rejected the idea that worldviews could or should be as easily separated as institutions.

The theoretical shift from ultimate to more proximate concerns also confronted Kuyper in the work of modernist theologians, the original secularization theorists. Allard Pierson and L. W. E. Rauwenhoff, following the example of German theologian Richard Rothe, expected humanity to reach its zenith through modern society and not through the church. The church was an obsolete medieval vestige in modern society. With social functions such as education and welfare taken up by the state, modernists asked what need there was for a church. Rauwenhoff explained: "What actually lays in the beautiful dream of the Kingdom of God on earth can be fulfilled in and through the state" (Augustijn 1986: 58). Although secularization as the decline of religion did not occur on a wide scale in nineteenth-century Netherlands, this kind of thinking did lead to a small but highly publicized decline, since several of these theologians carried their conclusions to their logical end and left the church, including Allard Pierson, F. Domela Nieuwenhuis, and C. B. Huet. Pierson's departure in particular plagued Kuyper for several years.

III. Covenant Theology for a Secular Society

Kuyper's covenant theology was a tool for *and* against these different aspects of secularization. The decoupling of the church and state by the 1848 constitution and its practical outworking posed an identity crisis for the *volkskerk*, as one might imagine would happen when, to take the example of the *duplex ordo* system, a religious community loses control over its own religious text to the state. Historians Joris van Eijnatten and Fred van Lieburg conclude, "Orphaned by the withdrawing of the state and no longer obvious symbol of the existing order, [the church] needed a new legitimation" (van Eijnatten and van Lieburg 2005: 271). Kuyper's *Doctrine of the Covenants* provided just that.

Kuyper argued that this crisis in the church was, in part, a crisis of covenantal awareness. "Satan has enticed the church onto these one-sided paths, has undermined sacred baptism, and has dug away the only foundation on which a healthy church-life can bloom exactly through this adroit expulsion of the truth of the covenant" (Kuyper 1909: 8). Kuyper's covenant theology accomplished two important tasks. While modernists counted the value of the church in terms of its practical social function, Kuyper argued that the church had a divine mandate founded in God's covenant. Second, if the church was no longer a state church, the boundary lines had to be redrawn. Church membership could no longer be a reflex of citizenship. Kuyper argued that the covenant was the proper basis for distinguishing who belonged in and who did not.

The immediate impetus for Kuyper's articles on covenant illustrates the predicament in which he found himself, between modernist theologians on one side and conservatives on the other. Kuyper wrote these articles at the request of J. W. Felix, curator of the Free University, to prove his worthiness for the chair of dogmatic theology. Some, like Felix and perhaps Philip Hoedemaker, were concerned that Kuyper's free church vision was a bit too modern and his recent series on particular grace potentially individualistic and sectarian (Stellingwerff 1987: 109; Aalders 2005: 31-32). To prove his worthiness as a Reformed dogmatician, Kuyper was asked by Felix to write on the doctrine of the covenant. Such concerns were one reason why Kuyper focused on the covenant as the basis for the unity of the church over against sectarian views, which grounded the church in one link or another of the *ordo salutis.*

The sectarian approach was embodied by the Labadists, who believed that the church was made up only of the truly regenerate or truly elect. Kuyper especially resisted this sectarian approach in the section devoted to the question of the boundaries of the church, later entitled "The Members of the Covenant." In this section Kuyper rejected the sectarian qualification for church membership and conversion, and moreover, election was no better. "Neither the middle nor the very first nor any link in the golden chain of salvation can bring us farther" (Kuyper 1909: 176; see also 194-96).

In fact, Kuyper argued that election had no practical value for the church. Instead he defined the church on the basis of the covenant: "God has bestowed his covenant on us so that we, distinguishing according to that Covenant, would escape the dangers which every other division brings with it, and yet avoid identification with the world" (177; see also 179). Covenant was the basis for distinction between God's people and the world. Covenant members were distinguished according to their "word and deed, or in other words their confession and walk, or their doctrine and life" (185; see also 192). The church cannot judge the internal state, but rather "the church must treat each external covenant member, so long as he can maintain his position as external covenant member, 'as though he actually was' what he perhaps indeed is not" (187). Kuyper's covenant theology thereby avoided the sectarian error of trying to determine some aspect of God's inscrutable counsel, yet Kuyper's insistence on discipline and a judgment of Christian character also did not take church membership for granted, as did the *volkskerk*.

The *volkskerk* (the Netherlands Reformed Church) was the church of the Dutch nation, and membership between either community was virtually interchangeable, at least for the Protestant portion of the population. Kuyper had long objected to the broadness of the *volkskerk* and its bloated membership roles, and he insisted that some distinction must be made between the true and the nominal members of the church. In *Church Visitation at Utrecht* (1868), for example, Kuyper protested against the common practice of allowing all and sundry to bring their children for baptism regardless of their Christian testimony. Kuyper wanted a church of sincere believers. In the context of the separation of church and state, Kuyper's covenantal ecclesiology transformed the church into a voluntary institution.

This voluntary approach, however, potentially conflicted with the Reformed practice of infant baptism. How could the central place of organic communities such as families be maintained alongside the demand for sincerity of individual confession and also the proper limited sphere of the church? Kuyper answered that the covenant was made with organic communities, not merely individuals. Kuyper followed the eighteenth-century Dutch divine J. C. Appelius and insisted that the covenant was not with the individual but with the church corporate. Baptism, the sacrament of the covenant, was not for the children as individual Christians but as members of the church, and further spiritual life was a product of covenant membership, not vice versa (see Kuyper 1909: 197-207). Thus Kuyper maintained a voluntary ecclesiology but also the practice of including children in the church, even those who may not yet have faith in Christ.

Besides defining the boundaries of the church, covenant also provided the legitimacy that the church desperately needed in the face of modernist criticisms that the church was an obsolete medieval appendage. The covenant as the divine source of the church persisted through all ages. "The warp and woof in the whole relation of God to the church of the Old Testament, both under the patriarchs and in Israel's days, is always the same covenant of fidelity that Jehovah had made with the church" (159). Specifically, the emphasis was on the external covenant as the source of the institutional church. The external covenant established the institutional church as a means and instrument of salvation, and as such it made the church its own life-sphere: "It pleased God the Lord to bring his Covenant of Grace in this life also to an external form and to use it in that form as means and instrument 1. to create for his elect a livable life-terrain [i.e., a 'life-sphere'], free from that all too terrible godlessness; 2. to treat his elect with common and saving grace; 3. to spiritually prove, to enrich, to sanctify, and to glorify his elect who came to life; and 4. to judge the consciences of many of them who resist faith in the Lord Jesus Christ" (185). Though the state was gradually encroaching on the church's traditional roles such as education and poor relief, the church's function as God's means of grace assured its continuing importance for humanity.

The Doctrine of the Covenants began as a series of newspaper articles in the fall of 1880, the same fall that Kuyper gave his famous inaugural lecture for the Free University of Amsterdam, "Sphere Sovereignty." "Sphere Sovereignty" was a baptized vision of the modern differentiated society. Each sphere — education, government, religion — had its own autonomous scope and function. Each sphere was controlled by its own unique "laws of life," yet each sphere still operated under the sovereignty of God. In Kuyper's vision of a society composed of distinct autonomous spheres, covenant had a double function, both delimiting the proper sphere of the church and explaining its unique function.

A bit of contrast brings out the salience of Kuyper's covenant theology for the modern era. Puritans in old and New England, including Jonathan Edwards (as Harry Stout has shown), also held firmly to the covenant of grace, and it was intertwined with their belief in a national covenant. As Stout explains, "One covenant — the 'covenant of grace' — referred to individuals and personal salvation in the life to come. The other covenant — the national covenant — applied to nations and governed their temporal success in this world. In early Puritanism these two contradictory covenants — one of faith, the other of works . . . existed in creative tension" (Stout 1988: 143; see also Vallance 2005). For these Puritans, the new nation inherited the promises to Israel. Kuyper's covenant theology, on the other hand, severed the link between the covenant and the nation, calling into question the premise of the *volkskerk*. Kuyper's covenant theology cut off that portion of the *volkskerk* population whose membership in the *volkskerk* was more a reflex of membership in the Dutch nation than personal faith. Kuyper's covenant was not, therefore, a foundation for the nation but for the church. Of course, in Kuyper's own day it was those like his Free University colleague Philip Hoedemaker, not the American Puritans, whose ideas of a national covenant Kuyper resisted. Over against Kuyper, Hoedemaker maintained the *volkskerk* ideal: "The whole church for the whole of the nation!"

This experiment in modern theology has useful implications for understanding and applying Kuyper's theology. For one, it suggests that Kuyper's oft-repeated dictum, "there is not a thumb's breadth in the whole domain of our human existence over which Christ, who is Sovereign over all, does not cry: 'Mine!'" was not the thesis of his speech but rather something more like a concession (Kuyper 1880b: 35). It was certainly a nod toward Antirevolutionary principles and the conservatives in the audience, but as George Harinck has pointed out, the accent in "Sphere Sovereignty" lay not on the unity but on the differentiation of society (Harinck and Winkeler 2006: 701).

This matches the observations here that Kuyper was at this time primarily concerned with disentangling the spheres of society, especially the church sphere, through his covenant theology. "No square inch" — really an unremarkable observation coming from a Calvinist — was an assurance to his audience that he had not left his Calvinistic inheritance behind while he was appropriating concepts like separate societal spheres and organic laws of life, which were certainly not the bequeathal of Calvin. Such an assurance was necessary. It anticipated the objections of both conservatives and modernists who thought "Sphere Sovereignty" had clearly departed from Calvin and adopted modern modes of thought. The emerging dilemma for Kuyper — and indeed for much of modern theology — was how to defend the continuing uniqueness of the church and still retain some kind of Christian public witness. In 1880, it was still unclear how this would work out.

This dilemma still plagues some of Kuyper's followers. In a recent issue of the neo-Calvinist journal *Perspectives,* Steve Mathonnet-VanderWell points out a few of the problems from which neo-Calvinism suffers, including a distressingly low view of the church. "Instead of being a unique body, the strange way God has chosen to be present and move in today's world, in neo-Calvinism, the church too often plays the subservient donor to creation and culture" (Mathonnet-VanderWell 2008: 14). Nicholas Wolterstorff says "Amen" to that (Wolterstorff 2008: 17-19).

If this diagnosis is indeed valid, the cure may not be as radical as abandoning Kuyper's heritage but, in fact, returning to it. "Not one square inch . . ." has become a banner for a church vigorously engaged in society. The irony is that a church separate from society was what Kuyper himself wanted. Beginning with his pastoral career at Beesd in the 1860s, to his involvement into ecclesiastical politics in the early 1870s and his 1880 treatise on covenant theology, Kuyper continually criticized the modernists who wanted to erase the line between church and society and the conservatives who capitulated too much to society and custom. Kuyper's covenant theology checked the temptation to subordinate the church to culture. The uniqueness of Kuyper's proposal was the argument for a differentiated society that nonetheless did not limit God's sovereignty. Covenant was a key component in this delicate balance. It explained why the church could not be sidelined as cultural cheerleader. Though God was sovereign over all the spheres, his sovereignty over the church was uniquely through the covenant of grace.

References

Aalders, Maarten. 2005. *125 Jaar Faculteit Der Godgeleerdheid Aan De Vrije Universiteit.* Meinema: Zoetemeer.

Augustijn, Cornelis. 1986. "Kerk En Godsdienst 1870-1890." In *De Doleantie Van 1886 En Haar Geschiedenis,* edited by Wim Bakker, pp. 41-75. Kampen: Kok.

Casanova, José. 1994. *Public Religions in the Modern World.* Chicago: University of Chicago Press.

Chadwick, Owen. 1975. *The Secularization of the European Mind.* Gifford Lectures in the University of Edinburgh for 1973-74. Cambridge: Cambridge University Press.

Harinck, George, and Lodewijk Winkeler. 2006. "De Negentiende Eeuw." In *Handboek Nederlandse Kerkgeschiedenis,* edited by Herman J. Selderhuis, pp. 597-721. Kampen: Kok.

Kuyper, Abraham. 1868. *Kerkvisitatie Te Utrecht in 1868 Met Het Oog Op Den Kritieken Toestand Onzer Kerk.* Utrecht: J. H. van Peursem.

———. 1880a. "De Theologische Faculteit En De Kerk." In *"Strikt Genomen." Het Recht Tot Universiteitstichting Staatsrechtelijk En Historisch Getoetst,* pp. 207-16. Amsterdam: J. H. Kruyt.

———. 1880b. *Souvereiniteit in Eigen Kring. Rede Ter Inwijding Van De Vrije Universiteit, Den 20sten Oktober 1880 Gehouden, in Het Koor Der Nieuwe Kerk Te Amsterdam.* Amsterdam: J. H. Kruyt.

————. 1890. *Is Er Aan De Publiek Universiteit Ten Onzent Plaats Voor Een Faculteit Der Theologie?* Amsterdam: J. A. Wormser.

————. 1909. *De Leer Der Verbonden.* Vol. 5, *Uit Het Woord.* 6 vols. Stichtelijke Bijbelstudiën. Kampen: Kok.

Mathonnet-VanderWell, Steve. 2008. "Reformed Intramurals: What Neo-Calvinists Get Wrong." *Perspectives* 23, no. 2, pp. 12-16.

McLeod, Hugh. 2000. *Secularization in Western Europe, 1848-1914.* New York: St. Martin's Press.

Sommerville, C. John. 1998. "Secular Society/Religious Population: Our Tacit Rules for Using the Term 'Secularization.'" *Journal for the Scientific Study of Religion* 37, pp. 249-53.

Stellingwerff, Johannes. 1987. *Dr. Abraham Kuyper En De Vrije Universiteit.* Kampen: Kok.

Stout, Harry S. 1988. "The Puritans and Edwards." In *Jonathan Edwards and the American Experience,* edited by Nathan O. Hatch and Harry S. Stout, pp. 142-59. New York: Oxford University Press.

Vallance, Edward. 2005. *Revolutionary England and the National Covenant: State Oaths, Protestantism, and the Political Nation, 1553-1682.* Woodbridge: Boydell.

Van Eijnatten, Joris, and Fred van Lieburg. 2005. *Nederlandse Religiegeschiedienis.* Hilversum: Verloren.

Wolterstorff, Nicholas. 2008. "In Reply (to Steve Mathonnet-VanderWell, 'Reformed Intramurals: What Neo-Calvinists Get Wrong')." *Perspectives* 23, no. 2.

Neo-Calvinism and the Welfare State

George Harinck

In talking about neo-Calvinism in the country where it originated, the Netherlands, two aspects must be kept in mind. The first is that the remarkable impact of neo-Calvinism in Dutch society in the twentieth century does not reflect the number of neo-Calvinists living in the Netherlands. Strictly speaking, neo-Calvinists were those who belonged to the Reformed churches, and they accounted for about 8 percent of the Dutch population. Of course, there were Dutchmen from other denominations who sympathized with the neo-Calvinists — in politics, for example — but since the introduction of the electoral system of proportional representation in 1917, their Antirevolutionary Party never won more than 17 percent of the vote in national elections. In the 1950s and 1960s, when the welfare state came into being in the Netherlands, at best the Antirevolutionary Party attracted about 10 to 12 percent of the vote (Harinck, Kuiper, and Bak 2001: 239-80).

Yet, small though their numbers may have been, the influence of the neo-Calvinists was large. They had the second-largest Protestant church in the Netherlands, with a much larger church attendance and much higher birthrate than the largest Protestant church (Selderhuis 2006: 781-843), and dominated the Christian labor union for many years (Werkman 2007: 218-55). Apart from the first seven years after the Second World War, the Antirevolutionary Party participated in every coalition government since the introduction of general suffrage in 1917. And a quarter of the Dutch prime ministers in the twentieth century came from a neo-Calvinist background.

These impressive figures must be understood against the fact that, in the twentieth century, the Netherlands had no majority group but consisted of minorities only. Of these, Catholics formed the largest minority — about 40 percent of the Dutch population in the 1950s and 1960s (van Eijnatten and van Lieburg 2005: 331). Catholics participated in almost every coalition government during the twentieth century. The influence of neo-Calvinists went hand in hand with compromise. Such a large influence is possible only by acknowledging minority status. But the neo-Calvinists were willing to compromise because they did not strive for a Calvinist nation. They wanted a nation that would respect the freedom of all minorities without distinction not because they were a minority themselves, but because this aim was the essence of a Calvinist political program. They presented a Calvinism that was a safeguard of civic liberties (Kuyper 1998: 279-322).

The second aspect we have to keep in mind when talking about the neo-Calvinists and the emergence of the welfare state is the characteristic structure of Dutch society. There was a time when Abraham Kuyper, the main creator of neo-Calvinism, did aim to turn the Netherlands into a nation under Calvinist rule. But over the years the neo-Calvinists changed their mind. From the start of his public career in about 1870, Kuyper abandoned the idea of a privileged or state church and welcomed the separation of church and state wholeheartedly, defending free churches as a preferable ecclesiastical concept. But at first he did not abandon the idea of a Calvinist nation. He thought about creating within the state a distinct Calvinist minority in a distinct Calvinist church. This phalanx would then one day take over the liberal state and turn both state and society in a Calvinistic direction, that is, a culture "in which the Christian feels at home and in place, and one in which the atheist is constantly reminded of the undeniable fact that it is he, and not the Christian, who is the *exception,* and that though he too receives consideration, he does so only as an exception to the rule" (Kuyper 1880: 77).[1] In such a state, freedom of religion would be respected. Kuyper's model was the United States where, as he wrote in 1878, "on the one hand the government prays, ordains days of prayer, respects the seventh day, etc., and on the other hand the government is more impartial respecting the different churches than in any other country in Europe" (75).[2]

---

1. ". . . een inrichting [van de staat], waarin de Christen zich thuis en op zijn plaats gevoelt en die den atheïst steeds aan het onloochenbare feit herinnert, dat niet de Christen, maar hij de *uitzondering* is, en er dus óók wel op hem, ja, maar toch niet dan bij exceptie is gerekend."

2. ". . . waar men eenerzijds als overheid bidt, biddagen uitschrijft, den zevenden dag eert enz., en toch anderzijds zich neutraler tegenover de kerken onderling gedraagt dan eenig ander land in Europa" (text dates from June 3, 1878).

But Kuyper and his followers realized that this plan was not realistic, and in the late 1880s he left this idea behind and advocated a society that was pluralist in principle.

> The state says: I cannot leave the persuasions to themselves, because they don't have the means to work oneself up, and I am not allowed to choose for one party or the other, therefore I will choose the system of *parallelism,* I will lead them in parallel ways according to the system of *equality before the law.* Since 1889 [the first Dutch government by a Christian coalition, 1888-91] . . . we have come on a better way with this system. It is this system the present cabinet [1901-5, in which Kuyper was the prime minister] wants to prolong. It does not want to give precedence to this or that group, not to give up the unity of the nation, not to favor or undervalue, but offer the same opportunity to both antithetical parts, like the father of the house will support and help along both sons equally, although they differ in world-view. (Kuyper n.d.: 26-27, 55)[3]

This did not mean that he declared Calvinism obsolete in matters of state and society. Rather, Calvinism got a different function within state and society than he intended at first. The character of state and society would in large part depend on the character of the coalition government. But the structure of Dutch politics, and the structure of Dutch society, had to be organized according to a key principle of Calvinism, that is, the freedom of conscience, a leading principle in Kuyper's ideas on the state since the early 1870s (Bratt 1998: 279-322). The state should have no right to judge someone's religion or worldview, but should defend the freedom of any opinion under the law. This may sound familiar today, but there were all kinds of opinions Dutch liberals in the 1870s would never allow in the public domain. They did defend the idea that public schools should be neither Catholic nor Calvinist but neutral in character — which meant liberal — and they held that public debate should be based on reason and not on religious convic-

---

3. "De staat zegt: ik kan die richtingen niet aan zich zelf overlaten, want zij hebben geen middelen genoeg om zelf vooruit te komen, ik mag niet voor deze of gene partij kiezen, maar ik zal nemen het stelsel van *parallellisme,* ik zal ze beide evenwijdig laten loopen en volg zoo het stelsel van *rechtsgelijkheid.* Met dat stelsel zijn wij sinds 1889 . . . op een beteren weg gekomen. Het is dit stelsel, waarmede het tegenwoordige kabinet wil voortgaan. Het wil niet aan deze of gene groep den voorrang toekennen, niet de eenheid der natie prijsgeven, geen bevoorrechting of miskenning uitoefenen, doch aan de beide antithetische deelen eenzelfde kans laten, evenals de vader van het huis de beide zonen, al verschillen ze in levensopvatting, gelijkelijk zal steunen en voorthelpen" (December 10, 1904).

tions. On the other side of the political spectrum, the socialists aimed at a radical change of society, and in their society religion would not be accepted, even within the boundaries of the church.

Against both of these political visions, Kuyper positioned his own new vision, one that did not exclude religions and worldviews from the public domain, but invited them to realize themselves in the public domain. It was not reason, state, or law, but worldview and religion that were vital to sustain the public sphere. As Kuyper's coworker, the Antirevolutionary lawyer and politician A. F. de Savornin Lohman, wrote in 1901: "Contrary to what it is claimed sometimes, there radiates no invigorating power from the constitution. . . . That only radiates from the people and from the spirit that inhabits the people" (de Savornin Lohman 1901: 50).[4] Here there are echoes of Paul's appreciation of the law in his letter to the Galatians. By excluding religion from the public domain Kuyper was convinced his political opponents did nothing but frustrate the development of civil society, since it was worldviews and religions that were the key to a responsible citizenship and an active civil society.

The Catholics soon realized that their religion was safe with this ardent Calvinist and supported Kuyper, and over the years practical implications of Kuyper's ideas were widely accepted and became the foundational structure of Dutch society in the twentieth century. This society has often been characterized as a "pillarized" society, a description that lays stress on social structure. But behind this pillarized society lies the idea so dear to Abraham Kuyper of a plural public domain.

I. Social Laws and Personal Responsibility

The priority neo-Calvinists gave to civil society implied a minor role for the state. The state had to uphold law and order, and defend national boundaries. That was about it. But from the late nineteenth century on, state and society became more and more intertwined. For example, laws were introduced to regulate working hours, despite neo-Calvinists stressing the fact that it was not in accordance with sphere sovereignty for the state to regulate the labor relationship between factory owners and employees. Instead of introducing laws that would regulate social life directly, they were in favor of

4. "Van de grondwet kan nooit, zooals wel eens beweerd is, 'levensverwekkende kracht' uitgaan. . . . Die gaat uit van het volk zelf en van den geest die in dat volk woont."

social laws that would function *indirectly,* by requiring parties to cooperate and make deals. And when it came to social laws to secure payment for unemployed and ill employees, the neo-Calvinists favored an insurance system for which each employee had to pay, against a system in which the state supplied the money and thus functioned as a substitute to personal responsibility. So, when they made a new poor law in the 1910s, they gave priority to the church over the state in the financial care for the poor; state support was subsidiary. The social care provided by the church was based not on right, but on moral duty, and would thus keep alive the moral responsibility of the poor to care for their own (Harinck 1992: 55-57).

When Dutch society was confronted for the first time with the phenomenon of mass unemployment in the First World War, this priority turned out to be too idealistic. Yet the impulse behind this poor law is telling: the church should be protected from the growing influence of the state. In general, the neo-Calvinists were afraid that the state would take over functions proper to civil society. In the world economic crisis of the 1930s, this meant that the neo-Calvinist prime minister H. Colijn only reluctantly accepted the fact that the government had to pay the hundreds of thousands of unemployed, as well as invest in public projects to create new jobs. Colijn could only live with this idea as a temporary measure, and in fact preferred a general readjustment of the living standard to the lower economic level of pre-1914, rather than extensive state investment in the public sphere (Langeveld 1998: 257). The economic and political developments of the 1930s and 1940s in Europe were irreversible, however, and led to the introduction of the welfare state in the Netherlands after the Second World War. Colijn had been wrong, and neo-Calvinists had to find a way of accepting the state's social-economic function in society.

II. "Our Principles Are Not Trustworthy"

How are we to explain this social-economic outlook of the neo-Calvinists? Many aspects might be emphasized, but it is arguable that the neo-Calvinists were hindered by their idea of sphere sovereignty. In former times social care together with education had indeed been a function of the church, but in the Netherlands the differentiation of society had resulted in a shift in responsibility for education from church to state by about 1800. The same thing would have happened with the care for the poor early in the nineteenth century, if the Dutch church had not defended the status quo, protested and obstructed the ambitions of the state to control this domain as well (De Haan 2003: 24-35). By modernizing the social role of the deacons in society Kuyper reactivated the social role of the church in the late nineteenth century. He believed that the church should play an active role in civil society by administering social care. So, for example, the reformed deaconry in Rotterdam founded and ran a hospital. But it turned out that this idea was too optimistic. In the long run the churches lacked the money and the deacons, who voluntarily took their office in church but had their own jobs, lacked time and competence to run a complicated organization like a hospital (Bornebroek 1989). Kuyper had pleaded for full-time deacons, paid for by the church, just like the ministers (Kuyper 1883: 66). But this plan never was accomplished.

This is only one example out of many that showed the neo-Calvinists that their principles collided with the changing character of reality. From the 1920s on the intellectual circles of neo-Calvinists discussed the impotence of the Reformed principles, as expounded and interpreted by Kuyper. In 1919 Herman Bavinck, the leading neo-Calvinist theologian, stressed that Kuyper's worldview offered answers that fitted his system but did not match reality (Harinck, Kooi, and Vree 1994: 42, 50). Facts had turned out to be more powerful than principles. The time of principles was over. "In many respects we don't know what we are up to, the strength and the effects of our principles are not trustworthy," Bavinck declared (Anema and Bavinck 1915: 45).[5]

Religion being central to neo-Calvinism, union leaders and politicians looked to the theologians for a way out of this dead end. Between the first and second world wars they waited for their theologians to adapt Kuyper's views on the structure of society in ways that would address the present problems of modern society. But no answer came. I dealt with the reasons for this failure elsewhere (Harinck 2007), and now stress only that at the time the welfare state was introduced in the Netherlands by a coalition of social democrats and Catholics, from the late 1940s on, the neo-Calvinists had no alternative view to offer. The only thing they did was reject the growing influence of the state in society quite generally. The intellectual weakness of the neo-Calvinist position was revealed by the fact that they described one of the first social laws not based on the insurance system and generally offered to the Dutch citizens — the introduction of pension laws in the 1950s — as a

---

5. "Wij weten op tal van punten niet, waar we aan toe zijn, welke de draagkracht en straallengte van onze beginselen is."

step toward Stalinism or to a totalitarian state, and unbalanced opinion of this kind was very common in neo-Calvinist circles.

To many intellectuals this situation was unsatisfactory. After having waited in vain throughout the interwar years for the theologians to offer an alternative view on modern society, the neo-Calvinist labor unions and the Antirevolutionary Party founded their own research institutions that functioned as think tanks.

III. Church and Christian Organization

Before considering the outcome of this new intellectual investment, it is worth asking what happened to the church once the welfare state was introduced in the Netherlands. At one level, the end of the theologians' monopoly on neo-Calvinist social reflection and the start of intellectual reflection as a political party or a labor union was a congenial extension of the idea of sphere sovereignty. At the same time, this illustrates a weakness in Dutch neo-Calvinism. Kuyper's idea of sphere sovereignty in combination with his ideas on a plural society — resulting in the "pillarization" of Dutch society — had resulted in all kinds of neo-Calvinist organizations. While the church remained important to these organizations and to society in general, these organizations did not diminish its role, but after the First World War two changes occurred that led to a decline in the social role of the church.

In the first place, secularization came to Dutch society. There had always been nonreligious Dutchmen, but as a minority they had been almost invisible. Now their opinion was heard more loudly. In 1930 about 14 percent of the Dutch had no church affiliation (a high percentage compared to other European countries) and the assumption that the church had a leading role in society was challenged (Mikkers 2006). The churches were shocked by this development, but they were unable to address the question of how they might redefine their role in a partly nonreligious society.

Secondly, and related to the rise of secularization, European societies in general were confronted with the rise of totalitarian ideologies. Russia became communist in 1917, Italy fascist in 1922, Germany national socialist in 1933. To the neo-Calvinists, in a way these totalitarian ideologies looked like nineteenth-century liberalism occupying the public domain. But liberalism had respected religion outside the public domain, and never intended to dominate society and private life as well. These new totalitarian ideologies set themselves up as a substitute for religion, and aimed at restructuring every aspect of life. This totalitarian character was new and it caused the neo-Calvinists embarrassment. While some of them wanted the Antirevolution-ary Party to oppose national socialist and fascist political parties, others wanted the church to speak out, because these were ideological movements and not just political parties. But neo-Calvinists who adhered to Kuyper's conception of society opposed the idea of the church warning against cer-tain political parties, since this would be a confusion of spheres. The group that considered national socialism in the first place as an ideological move-ment won, and in 1936 the Reformed churches forbade its members to join the national socialist party. But it was a Pyrrhic victory. And the Dutch Re-formed Church, the largest Protestant denomination, did *not* speak out against national socialism in the 1930s.

This situation illustrates the problem the church had in defining its own position over against modernist ideologies, and at the same time shows a weakness in the Kuyperian societal structure. By delegating all kinds of func-tions in society to all kinds of organizations, the only function actually left to the church was preaching the gospel. When it came to the practice of Chris-tianity in society, the church was no longer needed or involved. The faction of neo-Calvinists that wanted a more central position for the church, and was successful for one time in 1936, turned out to be too small to set the agenda. At the beginning of the welfare state, Christianity was represented in the Netherlands by Christian organizations, not by churches.

This short digression helps us understand why it is no surprise that neo-Calvinist intellectuals bypassed the church after 1945 as they tried to adjust to the welfare state (Albeda 2004: 27-29). The church had failed to give an-swers to the social problems Dutch society had faced since the First World War, the theologians had not replaced the Kuyperian principles with a new format to relate church and society, and other organizations had eclipsed the church's presence in society.

IV. Dynamic and Progressive

As has been noted, after the war the neo-Calvinist organizations did not wait any longer for directives from the church or its theologians and invested in their own think tanks. Because the Antirevolutionary politicians resisted the decolonization of the Dutch East Indies (Smit 2006), resisted the introduc-tion of the welfare state (van den Berg 1999), resisted the Barthian critique of worldviews and the impossibility of Christian politics (Anderson 2006), and resisted the social-democratic invitation to Christians to join their party, there was a danger the party would become a political outsider. Neo-Calvinist intellectuals began publicly to repeat Bavinck's questioning of the reliability of the Kuyperian principles and complained that they were "empty boxes" (Zijlstra 1992: 19-20). At the same time, neo-Calvinist theologians abandoned social questions and concentrated more closely on religious and theological issues (Dekker 1992).

For a time this situation created a stalemate within the neo-Calvinist tradition, but the Antirevolutionary politicians realized that the resistance to every change and mere repetition of irrelevant principles was no alternative either. Something had to be done to relate the neo-Calvinist tradition to the real issues of a modern, dynamic society. In the 1950s some young intellectuals of the Abraham Kuyper Foundation, the think tank of the Antirevolutionary Party, started to distance themselves from the static interpretation of the Kuyperian principles that had prevailed since the 1920s. These young intellectuals were influenced by a former generation who had defended the denunciation of national socialism in 1936 by the Reformed churches. In keeping with this, they now proposed a more dynamic interpretation of sphere sovereignty.

Up to this point, boundaries between different spheres had been stressed, as well as the dangers of one sphere dominating the other and the tendency of the state to absorb functions of the spheres. But these young intellectuals, of whom Bob Goudzwaard was to become well known in the United States, stopped emphasizing the independence of the spheres and started to stress their responsibility instead. In this way, the idea of sphere sovereignty no longer simply prescribed a static structure for society, but was related to its dynamic direction. Applying these new insights to the role of the state in modern society, Goudzwaard hoped to break with the static way of thinking expressed by the use of the word "principle." The state did not have to stop before the sovereign spheres as if a wall separated state from society, or other spheres. Because the responsibility of the state for society was stressed — its tasks of keeping law and order, for instance — the function of the state was now formulated as defending and supporting public justice. And, depending on the circumstances, such a function may lead to the state's interference in any sphere (van den Berg 1999: chapter 4).

Depending on the circumstances, this dynamic aspect changed the idea of doing politics within the Antirevolutionary Party. Defending the sovereignty of the spheres in political debates had previously looked like simply checking the course of society according to known principles that are fixed and applicable in all situations, and was therefore not very challenging any-more. By accentuating the responsibility of spheres, politics became some-thing much more active, creative, and adventurous. The politician had to find out what the responsibilities of the different parties were in every new situa-tion. It was no longer fixed principles or tradition that determined Anti-revolutionary political choices. Rather, "Doing Christian politics means that we see and recognize injustice and hunt after justice," as Antirevolutionary political leader Bruins Slot stated in 1960 (van den Berg 1999: 178).[6]

What were the effects of this new approach to sphere sovereignty? There were mainly two. In the first place it diminished the explicit Christian charac-ter of politics. Previously, it was easy to get the impression that Antirevolu-tionary politicians claimed to know the real structure of society, and that this knowledge was hidden from those who were not neo-Calvinist. By stressing the calling of Christian politicians instead of fixed Christian norms, politics became a cooperative search for the common good and for justice. Christian politicians did not have all the answers, but they did know they were called to preserve and restore public justice (van den Berg 1999: 160-67).

Secondly, now that the emphasis fell on the vocation of Christian poli-ticians, Christian politics really became an activity, no longer something fixed, but a dynamic enterprise, focused on the development of possibilities that were stored in creation. Christian politics got a stronger missionary ap-peal. The new view on sphere sovereignty gave an impulse to the search for Christian answers to the uncertainties and tensions of modern society, like discrimination, poverty, and the nuclear threat. Apartheid in particular be-came a prominent theme. "The race issue is not rooted in God's ordi-nances," prominent Antirevolutionary Party member J. H. Bavinck (one of the few theologians active within the party after World War II) wrote in 1956. In relation to apartheid, sphere sovereignty was not an argument for the separate development of black and white people in South Africa, but rather the reverse: it was an argument to respect the diversity within society (Schutte 2005: 392).[7] Stress was also laid on the eschatological character of politics. The open end of modern society was an invitation to construct and strive for a society that was more just and more open. Government was the engine Christian politics had to use to create a just society (Kennedy 1995: 110-13).

6. "Christelijke politiek houdt in, dat wij het onrecht zien en herkennen dat wij jagen naar gerechtigheid."

7. "Het rassenvraagstuk berust niet op de scheppingsordening."

The result was a much keener appreciation of the role of the state in society. The state was the instrument by which a responsible society was implemented and upheld. It had to function as a protective shield for weak and vulnerable citizens. This meant that from now on the active social role of the welfare state got a Christian interpretation in terms of Kuyper's social leanings and Christ's words in Matthew 25:35, words that were often quoted by Antirevolutionary politicians in these years: "When I was hungry, you gave me something to eat, and when I was thirsty, you gave me something to drink. When I was a stranger, you welcomed me." The accentuation of responsibility in relation to the spheres also resulted in a plea for a more responsible society, including a new accent on the sharing of authority and property. The Antirevolutionary Party within a decade changed from a somewhat outdated and conservative political party to a modern and progressive one.

V. Conclusion

In retrospect we can say first that the change described here saved the idea of sphere sovereignty from becoming obsolete. Thanks to this dynamic interpretation of one of its key notions, the neo-Calvinist tradition entered a new phase. Secondly, the church played a remarkable role in this process of change. At first, reflection on modern society was absent within the church and the welfare state often was rejected outright. Then in the 1960s neo-Calvinist theologians made society a prominent theme — but only by distancing themselves from a static interpretation of their own tradition, an interpretation that had isolated them all too long from the society to which they belonged. So, since the 1960s the Netherlands has had a dynamic neo-Calvinist sociopolitical tradition without a well-functioning church or theology. As the world knows, the Dutch welfare state in the Netherlands in these years is one in which every social want is taken care of by the state, with the result that a church did not seem to be needed anymore.

The question that remains to be answered is this. If it is religion or worldview that sustains civil society, as Kuyper stated at the end of the nineteenth century, and as Goudzwaard restated in the 1950s and the 1960s, how long can a modern welfare state, and how long can Christian or neo-Calvinist organizations, do without a well-functioning church or religion?

References

Albeda, Wil. 2004. *Ik en de verzorgingsstaat. Herinneringen van Wil Albeda.* Amsterdam: Boom.

Anderson, Clifford Blake. 2006. "Jesus and the 'Christian World View': A Comparative Analysis of Abraham Kuyper and Karl Barth." *Cultural Encounters* 2, no. 2, pp. 61-80.

Anema, A., and H. Bavinck. 1915. *Leider en leiding in de Antirevolutionaire Partij.* Amsterdam: Ten Have.

Bornebroek, A. H. 1989. *Eudokia. Honderd jaar ziekenzorg als opdracht.* N.p.

Bratt, James D., ed. 1998. *Abraham Kuyper: A Centennial Reader.* Grand Rapids: Eerdmans.

De Haan, Ido. 2003. *Het beginsel van leven en wisdom. De constitutie van de Nederlandse politiek in de negentiende eeuw.* Amsterdam: Wereldbibliotheek.

Dekker, G. 1992. *De stille revolutie. De ontwikkeling van de Gereformeerde Kerken in Nederland tussen 1950 en 1990.* Kampen: Kok.

De Savornin Lohman, A. F. 1901. *Onze constitutie.* Utrecht: Kemink.

Harinck, George. 2007. *Waar komt het VU-kabinet vandaan? Over de traditie van het neocalvinisme.* Amstelveen: EON pers.

————, ed. 1992. *Diakonie in verleden en heden.* Barneveld: De Vuurbaak.

Harinck, G., C. van der Kooi, and J. Vree, eds. 1994. *"Als Bavinck nu maar eens kleur bekende." Aantekeningen van H. Bavinck (. . .) (november 1919).* Amsterdam: VU Uitgeverij.

Harinck, George, Roel Kuiper, and Peter Bak, eds. 2001. *De Antirevolutionaire Partij, 1829-1980.* Hilversum: Verloren.

Kennedy, James. 1995. *Nieuw Babylon in aanbouw. Nederland in de jaren zestig.* Amsterdam: Boom.

Kuyper, Abraham. n.d. *Parlementaire redevoeringen,* IV. Amsterdam: n.d.

————. 1880. *Ons program.* Amsterdam: J. H. Kruyt.

————. 1883. *Tractaat van de reformatie der kerken (. . .).* Amsterdam: Höveker & Zoon.

————. 1998. "Calvinism: Source and Stronghold of Our Constitutional Liberties." In *Abraham Kuyper: A Centennial Reader,* edited by James D. Bratt, pp. 279-322. Grand Rapids: Eerdmans.

Langeveld, Herman. 1998. *Dit leven van krachytig handelen. Hendrikus Colijn, deel een 1869-1944.* Amsterdam: Balans.

Mikkers, Tom. 2006. "Ongelovig en onkerkelijk tussen 1920 en 1940. Reacties op een vergeten uittocht." In *Tussen Augustinus en atheisme. Kerkhistorische studies 2006,* edited by Tom Mikkers and Ineke Smit, pp. 164-74. Leiden: Faculteit der Godgeleerdheid.

Schutte, G. J. 2005. *De Vrije Universiteit en Zuid-Afrika 1880-2005,* 1. Zoetermeer: Boekencentrum.

Selderhuis, Herman J., ed. 2006. *Handboek Nederlandse Kerkgeschiedenis*. Kampen: Kok.

Smit, Herman. 2006. *Gezag is gezag . . . Kanttekeningen bij de houding van de gereformeerden in de Indonesische kwestie*. Hilversum: Verloren.

Van den Berg, Jan-Jaap. 1999. *Deining. Koers en karakter van de ARP ter discussie, 1956-1970*. Kampen: Kok.

Van Eijnatten, Joris, and Fred van Lieburg. 2005. *Nederlandse religiegeschiedenis*. Hilversum: Verloren.

Werkman, Paul E. 2007. *"Laat uw doel hervorming zijn!" Facetten van de geschiedenis van het Christelijk Nationaal Vakverbond in Nederland (1909-1959)*. Hilversum: Verloren.

Zijlstra, Jelle. 1992. *Per slot van rekening. Memoires*. Amsterdam and Antwerp: Contact.

Neither Ignore nor Modify nor Disrupt: The Kuyperian Model of Deliberation as Applied to Same-Sex Marriage

James J. S. Foster

I. An Existing Kuyperian Debate

There is surprisingly little material in the academic literature directly addressing, let alone voicing disagreement about, same-sex marriage from a Kuyperian perspective. One helpful example of such dissent, however, occurred in the pages of the journal of Reformed theology, *Perspectives*. In a December 2002 article entitled "Homosexuality and Public Policy: A Challenge for Sphere Sovereignty," Fred Van Geest made a Kuyperian case against any governmental ban on same-sex marriage. Van Geest's article incited a response in the April 2003 publication of the same journal by James W. Skillen, president of the Center for Public Justice. An examination of Van Geest's argument and Skillen's critiques can helpfully bring to light two points of tension between them.

Van Geest begins his argument against governmental bans on same-sex marriage by differentiating the Kuyperian model of the state from liberal and theocratic models. These latter models hold that the state has no right to enforce morality and a duty to enforce morality, respectively. The Kuyperian model, by contrast, rests somewhere in between (Van Geest 2002: 6-7). According to Kuyper's third Stone Lecture, the state is but one sovereign sphere among several. The social spheres of the family, science, commerce, art, and education are independent of the state, which is to say, they do not owe their existence to it (Kuyper 2007: 90). Indeed, each sphere is independently sovereign, answerable only to the internal authority that God, by grace, placed within it. These social spheres come about organically, in that their structure comes directly from creation.

The sphere of the state, however, is a mechanical remedy for sin — an intervention of grace following the fall. Kuyper explains the state's mechanical nature by saying it has both a "shady side" and a "light side" (81). The shady side consists in its imperfect multiplicity. In a sinless world there would be only one state — the kingdom of God — and so the fallen world, broken into its multitude of nations, is not as it should be. Yet there is a "light side" to this multiplicity in that the existence of each state is the work of common grace. Instead of letting the world fall into anarchy, God, who is sovereign over all, has granted limited authority to the magistrates in accordance with his mercy and for his own glory. This limited state authority — that is, the sovereignty of the sphere of the state as granted by God — is, according to Kuyper, a threefold right and duty, which he explicates as follows:

1. Whenever different spheres clash, the state must compel mutual regard for the boundary lines of each.
2. The state must defend individuals and the weak ones in each sphere against the abuse of power of the rest.
3. The state must coerce all together to bear personal and financial burdens for the maintenance of the natural unity of the state. (97)

Van Geest does not explicitly reference Kuyper's enunciation of the state's threefold right and duty, perhaps because he assumes his audience is familiar with it, but it is crucial to the remainder of his argument. For one duty that is explicitly denied the state is that of general moral watchdog. Drawing on the limited and contingent nature of the state in sphere sovereignty, Van Geest argues that a state cannot limit the rights of those who sin, so long as that sin does not cause personal or societal harm (Van Geest 2002: 8). According to Van Geest, sexual intercourse between or among consensual adults of the same sex is just such a sin, and therefore for the state to deny inheritance, visitation, pension, adoption, or — crucially — marriage rights to same-sex couples would be to overstep its bounds.

In closing, Van Geest argues that although marriage within the church is an institution created by God (and, he seems to indicate, therefore unavailable to same-sex couples within the Reformed tradition), "marriage means something different to the state" (10). To the state, marriage is simply a contract. Given the plurality of understandings of marriage in American society, there is no reason to limit access to this contract based on the Reformed tradition. Absent a public reason — such as harm to those who enter into or encounter same-sex marriages — to do otherwise would be as unjust as preventing the slothful from buying houses.

In his response to Van Geest's article, James W. Skillen accuses Van Geest of advancing not a Kuyperian argument but rather a "libertarian" one (Skillen 2003: 6).[1] Skillen concedes that the state is not an omnicompetent moral watchdog, but believes that Van Geest moves too quickly from individual freedom to state agnosticism regarding the nature of the social spheres. According to Skillen, in a properly Kuyperian understanding the state "should protect not only the rights of individuals, but also the rights of families, churches, schools (and more), each with its own kind of responsibility. For government to do justice to this complex diversity, its public policies need to uphold 'structural' as well as 'confessional' pluralism" (6-7).

Skillen's point is that the state cannot leave decisions regarding the nature of the spheres up to individuals. Rather, it must make a decision about what traits properly constitute a school, a business, a family, etc. A citizen does not simply enter into these spheres by fiat, for each sphere has its own created order that binds and constrains it.

Skillen concludes his response by arguing that same-sex unions cannot be properly considered marriage because they neither conform to historical pattern nor include procreational possibilities. Lacking the structural and historical similarity to heterosexual unions, same-sex marriages are in fact an impossibility. The state therefore no more oversteps its boundaries in prohibiting them than it does when it revokes the credentials of a school that has stopped teaching students in favor of selling cars.

Stepping back from this exchange, we clearly see the areas of agreement and conflict. Van Geest and Skillen agree that the state's power is significantly limited by the sovereignty of the societal spheres. However, they disagree about two critical points. First, Van Geest and Skillen have different views on the conditions necessary and sufficient to call a relationship a "marriage." For Skillen, certain historical and biological frameworks are controlling, while for Van Geest, these constraints are inadequate, especially in light of the plurality of definitions actually held in Western society today

---

1. Skillen does not explain what he means by a "libertarian" position beyond noting that it values individual autonomy and does not permit religious reasons to serve as the basis for prohibitions enforced by the state. As we will see, the position of "political liberalism," as defined in this paper, shares these two defining traits. Thus, for the remainder of this paper I shall assume that Skillen means that Van Geest holds what will later be defined as a "liberal" concept of the state.

(Van Geest 2002: 9). Second, they are at odds over how the state should decide what conditions it recognizes as necessary and sufficient. This second disagreement flows directly from the first. For Skillen, the proper structure of marriage is ascertainable through natural law and history, and it is therefore the duty of the government to recognize and uphold its boundaries. For Van Geest, the definition of marriage is in debate. Thus, the state is required to supply as broad a definition of marriage as possible so as not to prejudge in favor of one perspective (9).

Although adjudicating the first point of tension between Van Geest and Skillen is a worthy goal, it is a lofty one far outside the possibilities of this paper. The second point of tension, however, is far more easily addressed. In addition, by discovering whether Van Geest is truly Kuyperian in his approach to state recognition of same-sex marriage or, as Skillen asserts, liberal, a model for tackling the first point in a Kuyperian fashion comes into view. To make this judgment we now turn to Nicholas Wolterstorff's enunciation of Kuyperian deliberation.

II. A Model of Kuyperian Deliberation

In a paper given at the centennial celebration of Kuyper's Stone Lectures held at Vrije Universiteit, Nicholas Wolterstorff contrasted the Kuyperian model of public deliberation with what he described as the currently dominant model in the United States — political liberalism (Wolterstorff 1999: 190). While he conceded that this latter model incorporates a tradition too broad and multivocal to be easily categorized, Wolterstorff provided seven paradigmatic theses embraced by most forms of liberalism. Although each thesis is useful for a comparison to Kuyperian deliberation, four in particular are especially helpful for adjudicating between Skillen and Van Geest on the second point of tension listed above. Using Wolterstorff's numbering, these theses are:

1. Every normal adult human being has an equal pre-legal right to liberty of conscience and to liberty of non-harming action.
4. All normal adult citizens have an equal right to participate in the debates concerning [the] scheme of legal rights [in their society], and an equal voice in the making of decisions.
5. Citizens must be prepared to conduct their public debates concerning the scheme of constitutional and legal rights, and to make their deci-

sions concerning that scheme, on the basis of the deliverances of some source of relevant principles which is not only independent of all the comprehensive religious and philosophical perspectives to be found in society, but is one to which all normal adult citizens . . . can rightly be required to appeal for this purpose.

6. Government, in its interaction with the religions of the populace, must not do anything which has as its purpose or primary effect to aid some religion . . . nor anti-religious group. (191)

Wolterstorff calls the fifth thesis the "independent basis" thesis. This thesis significantly constrains the kinds of reasons that are eligible to be advanced in the public deliberation guaranteed by the fourth thesis. Further, it serves as justification of the sixth thesis; for there are prima facie no principles independent of religious or philosophical perspectives that call for promoting or discouraging certain religious or philosophical perspectives, so long as they do not violate the nonharm clause of the first thesis. According to Wolterstorff, the basic justification for the fifth thesis — and therefore also the constraints it places on the citizens and government in the fourth and sixth theses — is one of respect, the idea being that a citizen's opinion is, in violation of the first thesis, unjustly disrespected if the state limits his or her liberty for reasons he or she does not accept (195).

As Wolterstorff points out, the fifth thesis absolutely requires that there *is* an independent and common basis for deliberation, for without one the whole system falls to pieces. Without going into much detail on the reasons why, Wolterstorff writes that Kuyper would "regard the 'independent basis' thesis of liberalism as nothing more than a wan and forlorn hope" because "reason is not up to the demands."[2] Kuyper was by no means postmodernist

2. One example of Kuyper's resistance to the concept of independent reason can be found in the fourth lecture on Calvinism, "Calvinism and Science." Here Kuyper sets himself against the "normalists" who

> do not rest until they have found an identical interpretation of all phenomena, and oppose with the utmost vigor . . . all attempts to break or to check the logical inferences of cause and effect. . . . [The normalist] tries to force *his* consciousness upon us, and claims that our consciousness has to be identical with his own. From this point of view nothing else could be expected. For if he conceded that there might be a real difference between his consciousness and ours, he would thereby have admitted a break in the normal condition of things. We, on the contrary, do not claim that *our* consciousness shall be found in *him*. (Kuyper 2007: 132, 137)

in his outlook — he believed that the world really was one way and not any other — but he held a pessimistic view of humanity's ability to ascertain and agree on its nature. In addition to finding the independent basis thesis fantastical due to the limits of human reason, Wolterstorff also notes another disagreement with this foundation of political liberalism. For Kuyper there simply are no ways of thinking separate from comprehensive religious and philosophical beliefs. Political liberalism treats such commitments as "add-ons" to basic rationality, whereas for Kuyper there are genuinely and holistically religious and philosophical ways of thinking (197). That is not to say that according to Kuyper every self-confessed Christian does think in a holistically Christian way, although each should. Kuyper acknowledged that for many people religion acted as an add-on. However, whenever religious commitments did serve as add-ons, they were being inconsistently bolted on to an existing worldview, not a freestanding rationality.

Based on these disagreements with political liberalism, Wolterstorff submits that Kuyper's model of democracy is similar to the modern deliberative model.[3] Like political liberalism, this model is more accurately described as a family of theories regarding the proper functioning of a democratic process, and therefore resists neat summarization. However, according to Wolterstorff, there are several commonalities among deliberative theories, two of which are useful here to contrast with political liberalism. Although the deliberative model in general agrees with the first and fourth theses of political liberalism, in contrast to the fifth and sixth these theses hold that persons are free to offer whatever reasons they desire in discussions regarding policies under consideration, and that a public deliberation should drive toward creating a just society, as opposed to one that maximizes individual liberty (200). The upshot of these differences is that, whereas political liberalism attempts to find consensus (or as near consensus as possible) based on a common rationality for the purpose of securing as much personal liberty as possible under the nonharm clause, deliberative democracy accepts disagreement as inevitable and attempts to give space for these disagreements to be debated in the public square, the hope being that this debate does not turn into a shouting match, but rather a shared quest for a just society incorporating citizens of different viewpoints. For the deliberative model to work, Wolterstorff notes, the minority view must submit to defeat at the hands of the majority, especially when one or more of their practices are found to be

---

3. Although he does not make it explicit, Wolterstorff is most likely pointing here to the kind of democracy described in his own work and that of Dewey and Stout.

unjust by the greater part of their fellow citizens, and their liberty to perform them is therefore constrained.

At the end of his description of the deliberative model Wolterstorff writes: "Kuyper is never . . . fully explicit about the model of democracy with which he is working. But I submit that if one assembles the things he does say, and extrapolates a bit, it becomes clear that this deliberative model is what he had in mind" (201). This is not, obviously, the strongest defense of a philosophical reconstruction ever offered. However, Wolterstorff's argument is bolstered by Kuyper's strong agreement with the deliberative model's two above-listed differences with political liberalism.

To give just one example of each, building on his aforementioned skepticism regarding a common, independent rationality, Kuyper rejects the exclusion of religious reasoning in the public square, writing in "Maranatha" that the state must honor religion because

> no authority or government can stand unless it finds support in *conscience*; lacking that it will *have* to find its strength in bayonet and pistol. . . . Positive government action in matters pertaining to our *spiritual* life is something we do not desire but fundamentally oppose. The gospel spurns the crutches of the powerful. All that it asks is unlimited freedom to develop in accordance with its own genius in the heart of our national life. . . . Only *this* we do not want: that the government arm unbelief to force us, half-armed and handicapped by an assortment of laws, into an unequal struggle with so powerful an enemy. (Kuyper 1998: 223-24)

Additionally, in the third lecture on Calvinism, Kuyper sets sphere sovereignty against that of "Popular Sovereignty, as it has been anti-theistically proclaimed at Paris in 1789" (Kuyper 2007: 87). While in popular sovereignty "the sovereign God is dethroned and man with his free will is placed on the vacant seat," sphere sovereignty "teaches us to look upward from the existing law to the source of the eternal right in God and . . . protest against the unrighteousness of the law in the name of this highest Right" (89, 90). Given these two crucial points of agreement, Wolterstorff's assertion that Kuyper was working with a deliberative model of democracy is by no means unreasonable. In addition, although it is anachronistic to attribute it to him, using the modern deliberative model is useful when considering what public discourse looks like in a Kuyperian state.

III. Kuyperian Deliberation on Boundary Conditions

With Wolterstorff's contrast between liberal and deliberative democracy, and his assignment of the latter to Kuyper, in hand, we are almost ready to return to the second point of tension between Van Geest and Skillen. First, however, one important aspect of Kuyper's understanding of the role of the state must be added, namely, the relationship between the social spheres and the sphere of the state. At first blush, and absent what Kuyper says that comports with the deliberative model, the threefold right and duty Kuyper enunciates in his third lecture on Calvinism appears remarkably compatible with political liberalism. Aside from protecting the boundaries of the spheres and collecting taxes, the only affirmative duty of the state is to protect the weak — to uphold something like the nonharm clause of political liberalism. It seems reasonable to argue, therefore, that the state oversteps its bounds when it prohibits the modification of a sphere — such as the family — by individual citizens for any other reason than protecting the weak or the boundaries of another sphere. That is, it would be contrary to the state's threefold right and duty to prevent same-sex couples from getting married — creating a family — because religious tradition holds that God disapproves.

However, this assertion turns out to be un-Kuyperian because it ignores the fact that the state's threefold right and duty is not freestanding. On the contrary, Kuyper couches the state's threefold right and duty within a larger, overarching duty — to "neither ignore nor modify nor disrupt the divine mandate, under which these social spheres stand" (Kuyper 2007: 96). This overarching duty is quite a vise. On the one hand, by Kuyper's lights, the state cannot engage in "positive action" regarding matters spiritual; but on the other, it has a duty to recognize the nature of the social spheres as divinely set. To thread this needle, it seems that the state must be importantly reactive. It must refrain from enforcing religious orthodoxy (or antireligious orthodoxy) while accepting the spheres as they are. This, of course, begs the question: How *are* the spheres, that is, what is, in fact, their nature?

For Kuyper, this question is perhaps not as pressing as it might seem. According to Kuyper, the spheres are organic entities that arise on their own as a result of the rules God has instituted over creation. In a sense, to ask "what is a church or a family?" is similar to asking "what is a grasshopper or a lake?" To a certain extent, this question can be answered merely by pointing to examples in the world and describing their characteristics. This does not mean, of course, that there will not be boundary disputes in the same way that someone might argue that a certain lake is really a pond. To reply to this objection, should one wish, one will need to first discern what is common among all lakes and all ponds, and then show how this body of water fits the criteria of the first more perfectly than that of the latter. In the same way, picking out the necessary and sufficient attributes of a given social sphere will be essential to solving boundary disputes regarding them.

Returning now to the disagreement between Skillen and Van Geest, it is apparent that their disagreement is, essentially, a boundary dispute. Van Geest believes that families can be founded upon the union of two same-sex individuals. Skillen disagrees. In addition to this dispute, Skillen also believes that Van Geest arrives at his conclusion regarding the boundary of the family sphere by un-Kuyperian means. Specifically, Skillen is concerned that Van Geest is arguing that "government should allow people confessional freedom to define marriage as they wish," denying government the "responsibility of making a structural prejudgment about what marriage is" (Skillen 2003: 7). In an author's response, Van Geest replies that he believes no such thing — that he does hold that the state has a responsibility to take a position on the necessary and sufficient conditions of marriage (Van Geest 2003: 8). Indeed, his whole point of raising the question of gay marriage was to initiate a deliberation about what kinds of relationships the state should identify as marriages. In other words, Van Geest's claim is not that the state should broaden its definition of marriage to include same-sex unions because he believes to do otherwise unfairly limits individual autonomy (a liberal argument). Rather, he thinks the state should recognize same-sex marriages because, contra Skillen, he finds them compatible with the proper understanding of the sphere of the family. In Skillen's defense, Van Geest does not clearly articulate this more nuanced position in his original article. Nevertheless, having clarified his position, it appears that Skillen is incorrect in labeling Van Geest's understanding of the state's relationship to the social spheres as too liberal to be properly Kuyperian.

However, Skillen is certainly not wrong, or un-Kuyperian, to enunciate his position regarding the proper structure of marriage. Indeed, nothing could be more Kuyperian than to enter into a public deliberation concerning which boundary lines the state should recognize for a given social sphere. Of course, having entered into this deliberative process, Skillen must be prepared to engage other positions on this issue. These positions not only include less restrictive views, such as Van Geest's, but also more restrictive positions such as those articulated in the state laws of Delaware, Maryland, and Virginia, which require a marriage be entered into in the presence of a religious representative.

IV. Conclusion

Hopefully, it will now be apparent why, as stated above, this paper could not arrive at a definitively Kuyperian definition of marriage. Although it is certainly possible to advance *an* account of the kinds of relationships a state should properly recognize as marriage, many accounts are available for consideration under a Kuyperian understanding of sphere sovereignty. As previously noted, that does not mean that there are not proper necessary and sufficient conditions for marriage, or that the structure of marriage is in flux, or that that structure is chiefly a product of social practices. It would be contrary to sphere sovereignty to assume anything except that marriage, being a part of the organic sphere of the family, has a divine order given to it. Still, because sin prevents human reason from achieving certainty regarding God's divine plan, ascertaining that order for the purpose of state recognition will have to be a product of a continual deliberative process.

There is, admittedly, an obvious criticism of this conclusion. Namely, that we need not deliberate about the proper structure of marriage as regards same-sex marriage in a Kuyperian context because Kuyper's position is clear. For example, in his meditation "Male and Female Created He Them" Kuyper writes that a creation including only men or only women would be "without marriage, without family-homes . . . without ties of blood, without wooing and repelling . . . one monotonous human sadness" (Kuyper 2004: 80-81). It is difficult to see how, given this understanding of marriage and family, Kuyper could find same-sex marriages as anything but absurd. Thus, to hold the contrary is of necessity outside the limits of Kuyperian thought.

However, to narrow inclusion in the Kuyperian tradition to mere repetition of Kuyper's position on this issue is undesirable for two reasons. First, as is well known, Kuyper's own understanding of the family changed in an important way during his lifetime. Late in his career, Kuyper modified his position on household franchise to include single women and female-headed households (Bratt 1984: 256). Compared to extending the definition of marriage to include same-sex couples, this may seem a small shift; but at the time, it was radical enough to precipitate a split in his Antirevolutionary Party. Second, it does a disservice to the originality and depth of Kuyper's thought. Through sphere sovereignty, Kuyper articulates a method of Christian engagement with the world that takes the limitations placed on human reason and achievement by sin seriously but also finds hope for progress through common grace. To dismiss positions that honor this model of engagement but do not agree with Kuyper's exact understanding of a given social sphere is to limit Kuyperianism to a small set of dogmatic positions. Indeed, if Wolterstorff is correct regarding the inclusion of comprehensive religious and philosophical perspectives in Kuyperian deliberation, such dismissal seems not only to unfairly constrain Kuyper's vision of the world, but to be positively un-Kuyperian.

References

Bratt, James D. 1984. *Dutch Calvinism in Modern America*. Grand Rapids: Eerdmans.

Kuyper, Abraham. 1998. "Maranatha." In *Abraham Kuyper: A Centennial Reader*, edited by James D. Bratt. Grand Rapids: Eerdmans.

———. 2004. "Male and Female Created He Them." In *When Thou Sittest in Thy House: Meditations on Home Life*. Wyoming, Mich.: Credo.

———. 2007. *Lectures on Calvinism*. New York: Cosimo Classics.

Skillen, James W. 2003. "Abraham Kuyper and Gay Rights." *Perspectives: A Journal of Reformed Thought* 18, no. 4.

Van Geest, Fred. 2002. "Homosexuality and Public Policy: A Challenge for Sphere Sovereignty." *Perspectives: A Journal of Reformed Thought* 17, no. 10.

———. 2003. "Author's Response." *Perspectives: A Journal of Reformed Thought* 18, no. 4.

Wolterstorff, Nicholas. 1999. "Abraham Kuyper's Model of a Democratic Polity for Societies of a Religiously Diverse Citizenry." In *Kuyper Reconsidered: Aspects of His Life and Work*. VU Studies on Protestant History 3. Edited by Cornelis van der Kooi and Jan de Bruijn. Amsterdam: VU Uitgeverij.

"Here the Shoe Pinches":
Kuyper, Tolerance, and the Virtues

John R. Bowlin

That Kuyper's understanding of sphere sovereignty recommends something like acts of toleration seems impossible to deny. One cannot assert a diversity of human goods, ends, and sovereign spheres of activity without also insisting, in general, on the need to tolerate the activities taken up and the ends pursued in each sovereign sphere. So, too, the need for toleration's patient endurance emerges from Kuyper's insistence that participants in different spheres proceed according to different material principles. By "principle" he means the collection of theological commitments, judgments about the good, and empirical claims that one takes for granted as one acts in this or that sphere, and he assumes that different principles generate specific differences among spheres of the same general kind (Kuyper 1998c: 484-86). Scholarship might be sovereign in its own sphere, but not all activities that count as scholarly have the same material content or social consequence, and the need for toleration accompanies the recognition of this fact. Referring to a life of scholarship governed by the Reformed principle — the one that accents a sovereign God who "stimulates life down to the root and overcomes all fear" — Kuyper writes: "We propose therefore to build alongside what others have built without anything in common except the yard outside, the view from the windows, and a press, which, like the mail, maintains the exchange of thought. For we certainly acknowledge that a battle of ideas is possible and necessary, again and again, but never over anything but starting point and direction" (486).

So long as there are sovereign spheres and so long as there is ontological multiplicity among them and principled diversity within, battles of this kind will be inevitable and the civil peace and social harmony that all desire will be regularly threatened by the prospect that ordinary cultural contest will take an extraordinary turn toward violence. And of course, it is precisely this inevitability and this threat that make the need for acts of toleration relatively constant. And if there is constant need, then it seems safe to say that Kuyper's account of sphere sovereignty recommends, not simply *acts* of toleration, but the habitual performance of those acts. It recommends, in other words, thinking of tolerance as a virtue. And of course, if tolerance *is* virtue, then it must belong to justice as one of its parts. Why justice? Because tolerance regards our response to the various differences and dissents that threaten to confound our various social and political relations, and justice is the virtue that in general regards the perfection of those relations.

This much is plain.

Less obvious is the fact that tolerance helps perfect relations with our own, with those we count in our own company. It is not, as so many assume, a virtue that governs our relations with strangers and aliens, that emerges only in the absence of social bonds and affections, or that inhabits the shadow world of liberalism, with its horror-flick collection of rootless individuals — the zombies of modern political theory. No, tolerance regards differences among those who already recognize each other as members of some social whole, and its acts are taken up, at least in part, for the sake of their life together. By these lights, tolerance emerges from Kuyper's account of sphere sovereignty precisely because he assumes an antecedent social bond that unites those who participate in the various sovereign spheres in a common enterprise. That antecedent enterprise is, of course, politics. Participants in the various spheres share a common political life and identity, and this gives them reason to tolerate some of what they find objectionable in the activities and principles of the various spheres. In the last analysis, sphere sovereignty creates a need for tolerance, not because it assumes an irreducible diversity of human activities, but because it asserts a unity that transcends our various differences. We tolerate what we might otherwise loathe because we already share a life with those who offend, because we recognize that they are ours and we are theirs.

Language, history, and ethnicity might mediate this shared political life and identity, this ground of tolerance, as they surely did in the Netherlands of Kuyper's day, but they need not. What matters is the shared political life, regardless of origin, which in turn not only provides reason to tolerate but also authorizes those charged with care for the good of the political community to regulate relations among and between the various sovereign spheres.

It enables the state to function as the "sphere of spheres," whereby it regulates and, no doubt at times, enforces regimes of tolerance, sphere to sphere (Kuyper 1998c: 468-69).[1] Of course, with this kind of power the state tends to overreach the bounds of its own sphere and encroach upon the sovereignty of others, and thus sphere sovereignty must always defend itself against state sovereignty (Kuyper 1998c). Still, a state that acts with just authority within its own sovereign sphere and gives expression to a people's political life, to their common loves, however slight, and shared aspirations, however slim, will also provide the framework for their mutual tolerance.

All these facts about Kuyper and tolerance are well known and require no further comment. Instead I want to consider the account of virtue in general that Kuyper assumes in his treatment of common grace. It is an account that, while not explicitly about tolerance, provides a framework for understanding some of the puzzles that confound our understanding of the virtue and some of the resentments that emerge from those puzzles.

If there is in fact a Kuyperian account of the virtues in general and of tolerance in particular, it begins, as Kuyper does, with the biblical drama of salvation and thus with his treatment of the vexing relations between nature and grace. In the beginning God created all things and called them good, set human beings in a garden, and ordered their lives, both interior and exterior, with "an environing and invasive grace" (Kuyper 1998a: 167). Adam's disobedience threatened disorder, ruin, and "death, in its full effect," but God intervened and bestowed a "common grace" upon nature (167). The principal activity of this grace "consisted in restraining, blocking, or redirecting the consequences that would have otherwise resulted from sin" (168). It "averted the lethal consequences of the curse and made possible and certain the continued, be it afflicted, existence of all that came from the original creation." With us now, this common grace guarantees the existence of created life and temporal history east of Eden, where human powers emerge, develop, and transform the exterior conditions of life and where virtue competes with vice within human hearts and across human history. And of course, this life and this history form the background against which Providence rules and saving grace redeems and re-creates (181). "The saved person is 'a new creature in Christ,'" and yet all along she

---

1. When language, history, and ethnicity mediate the political, immigrants will find it difficult to identify with that political community, participate in its common life, and participate in a regime of tolerance predicated on sovereign spheres. For an account of these difficulties in recent Dutch history, see Buruma 2006.

has been secured in being against the assault of sin by the common grace that bears witness to the glory of God (174, 168).

Some of what Kuyper says about the character of human life, virtue, and history under common grace must be refused. On this side of the twentieth century, both his insistence on inevitable progress in external affairs — in science, industry, and the arts — and his talk of inescapable decline in wisdom, love, and virtue seem equal parts wistful and naive.[2] The age between Pentecost and parousia is "not a blank space in the plan of God"; it does have "a purpose and goal"; there will be a "final decision," and presumably that decision will vindicate God's rule. Kuyper quite rightly opposes those who think otherwise. Yet these are matters of faith and hope, not knowledge and presumption (175). Augustine's just magistrate from book 19 of the *City of God* offers a better example. He admits that God rules history and that motive shapes human action, and yet he renders judgment in ignorance of each. Unintended harms follow in turn, and this compels him to his knees. At the end of the day, he prays for deliverance and perseveres in hope, but he claims

---

2. On progress Kuyper writes: "Common grace opens a history, unlocks an enormous space of time, triggers a vast and long-lasting stream of events, in a word, precipitates a series of successive centuries. If that series of centuries is not directed toward an endless, unvarying repetition of the same things, then over the course of those centuries there has to be constant change, modification, transformation in human life. Though it pass through periods of deepening darkness, this change has to ignite ever more light, consistently enrich human life, and so bear the character of perpetual development from less to more, a progressively fuller unfolding of life. If one pictures the distance that exists even now between the life of a Hottentot in his kraal and the life of a highly refined family in European society, one can measure that process in the blink of an eye. And though people imagine at the end of every century that its progress has been so astonishing that further progress can hardly be imagined, every century nevertheless teaches us that the new things added each time surpass all that has been imagined before" (Kuyper 1998a: 174). That ideas of progress come packaged with a certain relish for one's own and a certain disregard if not contempt (perhaps even racist contempt) for others should hardly surprise. As Kuyper sees it, this progress in science, industry, and material comfort will not be accompanied by moral and spiritual progress. Thus he writes: "But in the end it will not be these *two* operations which flourish to perfection in 'Babylon the great.' The glory of the world power which collapses in the time of judgment will consist solely in the second kind of development. Enrichment of the exterior life will go hand in hand with the impoverishment of the interior. The common grace that affects the human heart, human relations, and public practices will ever diminish, and only the other operation, the one that enriches and gratifies the human mind and sense, will proceed to its culmination. A splendid white mausoleum full of reeking skeletons, brilliant on the outside, dead on the inside — that is the Babylon that is becoming ripe for judgment" (181-82).

no knowledge of progress, he finds no evidence of decline (Augustine 1998: 19.6).

Other troubling features of human life under common grace are closer to what I admire. That God *uses* distresses, sorrows, and miseries as goads to virtue, that he *preserves* life under common grace as a kind of moral and spiritual boot camp, this, it seems to me, must be refused by faith in a God who is Love. At the same time, there is no denying that human life secured by common grace against chaos and death nevertheless abounds in difficulty and misery. Nor can it be doubted that the virtues are somehow indexed to these features. It's here, Kuyper insists, where virtue and suffering, providence and difficulty come together, it's here that "the shoe pinches" (Kuyper 1998a: 175). What we admire and praise about the virtues turn out to be inseparable from the suffering and difficulty that we would rather avoid. With Augustine's wise man, we might pray for deliverance from a life where virtue and suffering, excellence and difficulty are so tightly bound, we might lament this lot, and yet for Kuyper this prayer and this lot remain ordinary features of the virtuous life under common grace.

It is this aspect of Kuyper's social thought that I find both compelling and unavoidable. Here he stands in a tradition that goes back to Aristotle, a tradition that regards the virtues not as perfections of human agency *simpliciter,* but as perfections geared to the difficulties and miseries of human life. Excellence comes to our agency, if it comes at all, only in the context of struggle and woe, only as the virtues address the deficits, weaknesses, and uncertainties of human life as we find it — disordered by sin, preserved by common grace, and awaiting redemption and re-creation.[3]

All of this Kuyper assumes and all bears repeating as we consider tolerance. Why? Because tolerance, a virtue, is frequently counted among the vices, because it quite often elicits complaints and resentments, and because this response has something to do with these matters, with this relation between virtue and difficulty, or so I will argue. On the surface, most of us recommend a tolerant response to the diversity of ends and spheres, commitments and lives, but dig a little deeper and one finds discontent, widespread and growing. Left, right, and center, in our day toleration's critics are legion, all of them quick to point out the moral decadence and betrayal that toler-

---

3. One difference matters here. While the person of Aristotelian virtue will recognize the connection between virtue and suffering, excellence and difficulty without an eschatological horizon governing her judgment and hope, she cannot lament it, she cannot pray for its overcoming.

ance requires, or if not that, the condescension and judgment that the tolerated must endure.

A quick Google tour confirms both this surface praise and this deeper discontent. Web sites that praise the virtue and encourage its practice are countered by nearly as many that catalogue its stupidities and denounce its injustices. Conservative critics seem to make the most noise. Consider, for example, Bruce Bawer's remarks in his somewhat awkwardly titled essay "Tolerance or Death!" (Bawer 2005). I think he means "Tolerance *and* Death," but no matter. Here he argues that the species of tolerance that distinguishes liberal democracies is ill suited to our times. It's the virtue that enables the mullahs to preach hate and the terrorists to kill the innocent. In a similar vein, Mark Steyn argues that liberal democracies are incapable of acting with force and confidence when their way of life is challenged by moral decay from within and by unjust violence from without. Schooled in patient endurance, in easygoing open-mindedness, the inhabitants of liberal democracies — people like us, he means — tend to respond to these challenges by mustering ever more tolerance. Craven and foolish, they can't help but conclude that intolerance of other people's intolerance, other people's wickedness, is, well, simply intolerable (Steyn 2006).

Even its friends give tolerance only weak praise. Its attitudes and practices are useful, they say, perhaps even indispensable, for coping with disagreements and differences both large and small, and yet praise rarely proceeds beyond instrumental accounting. Tolerance is good because it helps us get along in spite of our differences, which is to say, in effect, that if we could get along without it, we would. A tepid endorsement indeed.

The standard explanation for both this explicit resentment and this subtle dislike goes something like this. Tolerance is unpleasant, both for those who tolerate and for those who are tolerated. Few of us want to endure the differences we dislike, and few of us want to be tolerated for differences we cannot forsake. The tolerant do not want to restrain their outrage and the tolerated would prefer to be accepted. The first act with regret and the second accept what is given with little gratitude. Both would prefer to live in a world where tolerance was unnecessary. Given this response, it's no wonder that tolerance is resented and its place among the virtues doubted. So goes the standard explanation.

But this can't be right. Justice is often unpleasant in precisely this way, and yet apart from the tyrannically vicious and the philosophically unhinged — apart from Thrasymachus and Nietzsche — no one resents justice *in se* or suggests that we remove it from our list of virtues. So the standard explanation won't do. Other sources of discontent with tolerance must be found, and one such source emerges as we attend to the relation between virtue and difficulty. To see how it does, consider the following opportunities to exercise neighborly tolerance.

An adult bookstore appears on your street, across from the public library and two blocks down from the post office and the middle school. Or suppose you live in Louisiana and your neighbor puts up a building in his back pasture and opens the Feathered Warrior Gamecock Club. Twice a month, people come from all over to place bets on roosters who peck and claw until one stands bloodied and breathless and the other lies dead in the dust. Or perhaps you live in South Florida and a Santerian priest moves in next door. He and his wife raise chickens, pigeons, and goats, not for their own consumption or companionship, but for ritual sacrifice, for the care and feeding of the Orishas, the gods of this world. It appears that the couple serves a small community of the faithful and that these bloody rites take place in their home, most likely in a basement room set apart for worship. Or, finally, suppose you live in rural Oklahoma, down the street from a Native American church, where some of your fellow citizens routinely ingest peyote in sacred ceremony.

Each instance, it seems, calls for the attitudes and practices of toleration. The activities in question — selling pornography, gambling, cockfighting, sacrificing animals, and using hallucinogens — are considered by many to be objectionable and are likely to generate problems of peaceful coexistence. At the same time, let's assume for the moment that they are not matters of "Civil Interest," as John Locke put it. They do not appear to regard those outward things — life, liberty, health, and property — that fall under the authority of the "Civil Magistrate." At the very least, they do not seem to threaten those civil interests and thus do not appear to be candidates for regulation by "the Laws of Publick Justice and Equity, established for the Preservation of those [interests]" (Locke 1983: 26). Rather, these activities appear to fall between the unbearably harmful and the harmlessly unobjectionable, the two extremes that frame the domain where acts of toleration might address problems of association. At the same time, George Fletcher speaks for many when he wonders whether this can be done, whether these activities can remain in this domain. By his lights, the psychological dynamics of tolerance and the slim history of its exercise should lead us to think otherwise. Those who, at first, muster some measure of tolerance in attitude or practice will most likely surrender to this dynamic and follow this history. They will either abandon their objections to what they at first found objectionable and muster some other attitude, perhaps indifference, perhaps acceptance, or they will take the opposite course and magnify their complaints. They will no longer consider the difference in question objectionable yet tolerable, but intolerably harmful and thus subject to the coercive force of law.

Why is this the likely progression of one's response to objectionable difference? Because tolerance is, according Fletcher, inherently unstable. At its core lies a psychological conflict that the initially tolerant soon find intolerable, insufferable. They must endure what they dislike and, all things being equal, would prefer to eliminate. Their objections quite naturally generate "an impulse to intervene and regulate the lives of others." At the same time, reasons of some sort convince them "to restrain that impulse . . . [and] suffer what they would rather not confront" (Fletcher 1996: 158-59). And, since all those who suffer quite "understandably prefer an easier way," the tolerant typically reconsider the objectionable activity or thing that requires toleration's painful act and relocate it among the unbearably harmful or the harmlessly unobjectionable — the two extremes that mark the outer boundary of toleration's domain.

Recent history seems to confirm Fletcher's hunch that tolerance is an unlikely and unstable answer to the problems of association posed by objectionable difference. Consider how recent responses to pornography tack between these two extremes while artfully steering clear of toleration's middle realm. Some have argued that pornography harms women precisely because it eroticizes inequalities of power. As such, it should be regulated by law, not tolerated by informal agreement (MacKinnon 1989). For a time in the mid-1980s, many found these arguments convincing. City councils in Minneapolis and Indianapolis passed ordinances that would allow women who believe they have been harmed by pornography to take civil action against anyone involved in its production or sale. But these ordinances did not survive First Amendment challenge, and even if they had, attitudes were changing. By the turn of the millennium, pornography and its milder cousins were ubiquitous, in most American homes just a mouse click or channel change away. Considered objectionable by most just one generation past, pornography has now become widely accepted, or if not accepted, at the very least an object of benign indifference.

Or consider the recent fate of cockfighting in the three states where it once flourished. Few regard it with indifference. In small towns and distant counties, many with Hispanic or Native American roots, cockfighting remains a noble activity, an ancient inheritance, and a mark of stubborn resistance against a wider culture that has little regard for rural lives and local traditions. In the suburbs and cities it elicits horror and, most prominently, embarrassment. One might think that mutual tolerance might address these differences to mutual benefit. It would enable one side to secure protection for a cherished tradition and recognition for the difference and merit of country life. At the same time, it would allow high-tech suburbanites and cosmopolitan city dwellers to retain their horror, while at the same time encouraging them to abandon their embarrassment. But the matter has resolved itself as Fletcher predicted. Citing the unacceptable harm cockfighting does to the roosters who fight and the subtle moral threats it poses to the citizens who watch, the state of Oklahoma banned cockfighting by referendum in 2002. New Mexico followed suit in 2007, Louisiana in 2008.

This desire to solve the problems of association that disagreement and difference pose without resort to toleration's patient endurance can also be seen in the Supreme Court's response to peyote use in the Native American church. As with cockfighting, what might be considered merely objectionable and thus potentially tolerable has been recast by legal judgment into the unbearably harmful and potentially suppressible.[4] But in other instances, this transformation has not been so easily made.

Consider the objections that Santerian animal sacrifice has elicited in South Florida. Harms have been catalogued and ordinances passed, but in each instance the courts have ruled against those who wish to restrict this activity, largely because the harms offered in justification have been both insubstantial and ordinary. In certain settings the animals used in Santerian sacrifice may well pose real threats to public health, but these threats so closely resemble those that accompany dairy farming and chicken ranching that one suspects that the ordinances were passed to suppress the merely objectionable, not the dangerously harmful.[5] Still, when the dynamic that Fletcher describes fails in this way, some other response to objectionable difference will no doubt appear, and if his hunch is right, it will not be tolerance. Indifference will grow, perhaps acceptance, and if neither of these emerges, then no doubt some other reaction will circumvent the suffering endured by the tolerant as they endeavor to do what, in the end, he insists they cannot do — restrain their desire to act intolerantly toward the activities they find objectionable.

4. See *Department of Human Resources of Oregon v. Smith*, 494 U.S. 872 (1990). In response to *Smith*, Congress passed the Religious Freedom Restoration Act of 1993, which was struck down by the Supreme Court in *City of Boerne, Texas v. Flores*, 000 U.S. 95-2074 (1997).

5. For the U.S. Supreme Court ruling on the effort in Hialeah, Florida, to ban animal sacrifice, see *Church of Lukumi Babalu v. Hialeah*, 113 Sup. Ct. 2217 (1993). See also Fletcher 1996: 163-64.

Surely there is some truth in what Fletcher says. Tolerance *is* difficult to muster. Objecting to this or that, wishing to intervene, and, at the same time, restraining that desire — this is, indeed, a painful and unstable state of mind. What's more, if Fletcher's remarks about tolerance are taken to be authoritative and exhaustive, then surely his account encourages its critics to complain. Objectionable difference abounds and tolerance is often recommended as a solution to the problems of association that follow in turn. At the same time, we are told that tolerant states of mind are unstable. They cannot be sustained. Those of us who try to sustain them eventually lapse into indifference or acceptance. These attitudes will, of course, generate tolerant *practices*. We will live and let live, but not because we have managed to combine objection and restraint, but rather because we believe nothing with conviction, or failing that, because we accept what our recent ancestors, courageous and upright, would have found abominable, intolerable. Either way, the tolerance we are encouraged to exercise in practice conspires against our own meager virtue and lands us in a contemptible nihilism, a traitorous moral flabbiness. On this account, tolerance is a kind of vice in disguise. It encourages us to keep company with the vicious even as we act among the tolerant. Given the praise it receives nevertheless, why not resent it? Add to these commitments and inferences the common belief that tolerance is found exclusively in modern, liberal societies, societies that some say encourage this kind of moral collapse, and this resentment is confirmed in a broader landscape of assumption and criticism.

Of course, these are not Fletcher's inferences and conclusions. He aims neither to praise nor to bury tolerance, but simply to point out its instability. Still, its most common critics assume that those who encourage tolerance of difference in fact recommend moral collapse, and Fletcher gives comfort to these critics as he confirms this assumption.

Now consider the other dynamic of impossible tolerance and objectionable difference that Fletcher describes, the one that leads to toleration's other boundary. Here, the objectionable but tolerable is recast as the unbearably harmful, and one might conclude, as Fletcher seems to, that this is simply the end of tolerance, and in a way it is. The difficulty of sustaining tolerant attitudes toward the objectionable does indeed lead to this recasting, and when successful, this recasting does indeed put an end to tolerance in both attitude and practice.

But in a way, this self-consuming dynamic is precisely what tolerance involves, or at least, this is what it is said to involve in Locke's famous explication and defense. On Locke's rendering, the objects of tolerance are all those activities and things that do not fall under the jurisdiction of the civil magistrate precisely because they have no bearing on those civil interests that he (or she) is obliged to preserve (Locke 1983: 39). Locke considers these activities and things indifferent, which is somewhat misleading, if not question begging. Certain individuals and communities might not be indifferent to some of the activities and things that the magistrate counts among the indifferent, but no matter. Indifference is indexed to civil interests alone, and this index determines toleration's scope. One might object to this or that, but so long as it shows up on the magistrate's list of indifferent actions and things, one may not respond with the coercive force of law. In these circumstances, tolerance is best. Of course, circumstances might change and what was once properly indifferent might be considered in a new light, and it's the magistrate's consideration that matters here.

Locke's example regards "the washing of an Infant with water." In itself, such washing is an indifferent thing, and thus one may not appeal to the magistrate for relief if one happens to object to the manner in which infants are washed in the church down the street. Normally, washing does not fall under the magistrate's jurisdiction. But not all times are normal. "If the Magistrate understands such washing to be profitable to the curing or preventing of any Disease that Children are subject unto, and esteem the matter weighty enough to be taken care of by a Law, in that case he may order it to be done" (40). In times like these, failure to wash, at one time an indifferent matter, is cast among the harmful.

Notice the fallout. Tolerance requires a domain of indifference, and on Locke's rendering it is the civil magistrate who determines its scope. As almost anything indifferent can become an object of civil interest, tolerance becomes a solution to problems of peaceful coexistence only as the magistrate's rule becomes potentially limitless. Given the right circumstances, communities and individuals can be denied their authority over any one of the indifferent activities and things that, given their other commitments, they hardly consider indifferent. For many, this conclusion quite obviously makes tolerance a dubious, perhaps a dangerous, solution to the problems posed by objectionable difference. And when this political dynamic is combined with the psychological one that Fletcher describes, tolerance becomes, for some critics, literally intolerable. By their lights, every defense of the virtue includes a subtle apology for potentially limitless state authority over human affairs. Toleration's advocates may not *intend* to extend the reach of state power in this way, but surely the tolerance they recommend generates this consequence by accident and in disguise. Add this unwelcome outcome to the impossible psychological demands that Fletcher contends the tolerant must bear, and a toxic mix emerges. Since these demands are escaped as the magistrate expands state authority over indifferent things, casts some among the unbearably harmful, and thus diminishes toleration's domain, those who try to muster toleration's painful act will be disposed to appeal for this kind of relief, which, for obvious reasons, the magistrate will be tempted to supply.

Of course, no one would accuse Locke of wanting to expand the reach of state power over the indifferent activities and things that most individuals and communities hardly consider indifferent; indeed, his aims were just the opposite. He wanted to safeguard local control and individual autonomy. Nevertheless, according to these critics, a political culture that embodies Locke's account of tolerance is too often despotic in consequence precisely because it grants too much authority to the civil magistrate over affairs that ought to fall under the jurisdiction of intermediate associations — families, churches, guilds, and so on.[6] Because tolerance emerges across the divide between the unbearably harmful and the objectionable but indifferent, and because it is the civil magistrate who specifies the character of this divide, presumably in accord with the state's civil interests, every defense of tolerance is in fact a defense of state power and of the conditions that might someday justify intrusion into the affairs of these associations. Equally troubling is the fact that toleration's domain will be as contested as political authority is. It too will be subject to the capricious, irrational, and often violent vicissitudes of power. Either way — either as pawn or as participant in power politics — it is not at all clear that tolerance can deliver what it promises. Its friends insist that it can bring civil peace as it secures freedom from state intrusion, but its foes have reason to doubt that it can.

Here, as before, Fletcher's aims are descriptive, not critical, and yet if his account of unstable tolerance is taken seriously, then, once again, his philosophical efforts provide cover for these complaints. And notice, once this cover and these complaints are combined with the praise that tolerance receives in societies like ours, resentment comes, it follows in turn. If tolerance amounts to *this*, this semblance of virtue and this threat to our authority

---

6. For a forceful statement of these views, see Conyers 2001. Of course, Conyers tries to imagine what an uncorrupted tolerance might look like (his concluding chapter is entitled "High Tolerance"), and in this union of complaint and revision his efforts resemble those of Budziszewski 1992. The trouble with both is that they justify their complaints with this or that account of tolerance and substitute their favorite alternative only as they mistake a semblance of virtue for the real thing. As we shall see below, it's a common mistake, this moral sleight of hand that follows Augustine's lead.

over ordinary associations, and if it is encouraged, practiced, and praised nevertheless, then surely we should not only oppose its practice and resent its praise but also resist the conditions — the diversity of life and commitment — that encourage our fellow citizens to commend it.

Fortunately, it is not at all clear that Fletcher's remarks exhaust all there is to say about tolerance or that the inferences its critics might make from those remarks are in fact justified. Consider, first, the psychological dynamic that Fletcher describes. Surely he is right. It *is* difficult to object and endure at the same time, and many of us will seek to avoid this difficulty by casting about for some other attitude toward objectionable activities and things. At the same time, it is not at all clear that this ordinary moral weakness warrants Fletcher's conclusion that tolerance is too unstable to recommend as one possible solution to the problems posed by disagreement and difference. If we assume that tolerance is a natural human excellence, if we place it among the other moral virtues, we soon discover that the psychological dynamics that Fletcher surveys are among the characteristics that distinguish virtue in general, not tolerance in particular. And if this is right, then Fletcher's doubts about tolerance are hardly warranted. So too, if this is right, then the inferences from difficulty to complaint and from instability to resentment are hardly justified. Or, put another way, if his doubts about tolerance are warranted because of the psychological dynamics it shares with the other virtues, then we would expect him to express doubts about justice, courage, and the rest, which of course he doesn't. We would also expect toleration's critics to extend their complaints and resentments to the other virtues, which of course they don't. If we place tolerance among the virtues, we soon discover that its instabilities are hardly unique, just as the moral traps it lays for those weak in virtue are hardly exceptional. At the same time, we discover that tolerance *does* have a special relation to its semblances, which, when combined with the psychological dynamics it shares with the virtues in general, does *indeed* generate unusual opportunities for confusion and thus for resentment.

Consider, then, the virtues in general and begin with Aristotle's authoritative account in book 2 of the *Nicomachean Ethics* (1104b5-1105a16). In general, each of the virtues fulfills roughly the same function. Together they perfect our ability to know, desire, and act for the sake of those things that are both choiceworthy and difficult to know, desire, and achieve. Were these things not choiceworthy, we would have no reason to love them or pursue them in action. Were they not difficult to know, love, and achieve, we would not need to be perfected by habit in order to respond to them well and pursue them in action. As we do many things, many habits are needed to perfect our agency, and each habit is distinguished from every other by the good it regards and the difficulties it addresses. Thus, for example, there is the good that can be achieved in human affairs when we give to others what is their due.[7] At the same time, most of us know what Aristotle's greatest interpreter points out: that it is often quite "difficult to find and establish the rational means" that would give to others what they are in fact due in this or that circumstance (*ST* II-II.129.2). For this reason we need the intellectual virtues, prudence in particular. By the same token, there are, as everyone knows, certain "obstacles to the establishment of this rectitude in human affairs," above all passions that too often confound our ability to judge well about the right and the good and that too often suspend our willingness to follow better judgment to right intention, sound choice, and praiseworthy action. For this reason we need temperance, courage, and the other virtues that perfect our relations to the various objects that elicit our various passions (*ST* II-II.123.1). And finally, most of us find it difficult to desire just relations in each of our many affairs with the constancy of habit, and it is for this reason that we need and praise justice.

Notice what follows once we grant that the moral virtues regard the difficult and the good. The virtuous are those who pursue the good — habitually, promptly, and with pleasure — even though difficulties of various kinds threaten to interrupt their pursuits.[8] This absence of instability is what their perfection involves, and this constancy of character is what it means to say that they are strong, that they act at the limits of their powers (*ST* I-II.55.1.1). The courageous, for example, respond well, not simply to ordinary difficulties and commonplace dangers, but rather to the most demanding difficulties and the most pressing dangers. Confronted with these graver threats, they respond with fear and daring in right order, which in turn enables them to judge well and to act for the sake of the good that they know to be best. The obstacles to right action posed by these threats and by the disordered passions they tend to elicit are, quite literally, overcome by the courageous, by their habitual disposition to respond in each instance with passions of the right kind and intensity. Indeed, for the courageous, these obstacles to just and praiseworthy conduct are hardly obstacles at all.

---

7. Here I follow Aquinas. See *Summa Theologica* I-II.60.2-3; II-II.58.3. Hereafter references to Aquinas's greater *Summa* will be noted in the text by *ST*.

8. Thus, if a person "stands firm against terrifying situations and enjoys it, or at least does not find it painful, he is brave; if he finds it painful he is cowardly" (Aristotle, *Nicomachean Ethics* 1104b7-8; hereafter cited in both notes and the text as *NE*).

By contrast, those of us with little or no virtue will not be able to respond as the courageous do, and for us the difficulties and dangers of this world remain substantial obstacles to the good we hope to achieve and the happiness we hope to have. When we are told we must be courageous and give virtue a try, we are put off by its rigors. More often than not, our meager, unstable virtue collapses under the challenge and we recast our account of the circumstances of choice and thus diminish our need for a virtuous response. We might conclude that the end we had hoped to achieve, the end that demands resort to courageous acts, is in fact a matter of indifference, not desire. Or, if that proves impossible, we might pursue this end but then insist that the unacceptable threats posed in its pursuit are in fact acceptable. The good threatened is in fact less worthy of our care and concern than we had first thought. Or, we might argue that the means proposed to achieve this end, means that present difficulties and dangers of various kinds, are far from best. Some other, less arduous means would be better. All these tactics are well known, all are designed to excuse us from acting as the virtuous do, all circumvent virtue's demands by deception, and all produce moral postures that are subject to unmasking.[9]

If this account is right, then it appears that instability afflicts every virtue that falls short of perfection, not simply tolerance, and this shared affliction appears to be an ordinary consequence of the difficulties that every virtue regards. Given this ordinary feature of the virtues in general, toleration's tendency to dissolve into some other moral posture hardly justifies Fletcher's doubts about the virtue as a source of civil peace. Courage, justice, and the rest display similar tendencies, and yet no one appeals to this fact in order to suggest that we can (or should) proceed without them. Rather, most of us acknowledge the difficulty of thinking, feeling, and acting as the virtuous do in precisely those circumstances of extremity that most urgently require virtue's act. Most concede that we fall short of moral perfection most of the time and that we squirm out of virtue's demands more often than we like to admit. Still, in a cool hour we recognize the virtues for what they are, for the goods they instantiate in themselves and for the benefits they secure

9. Recall how these tactics and postures were employed by the religious establishment of the American South during the heyday of the civil rights movement, only to be exposed as cowardice in the forceful replies of Martin Luther King, Jr. And of course, King's criticisms were effective precisely because most of us have little difficulty imaging the decay of virtue or seeing the difference between courage and its semblances once they have been carefully described and distinguished. See his April 16, 1963, "Letter from a Birmingham Jail" (1963).

when they succeed. In fits of justice and charity, we take note of those who lay hold of these goods and obtain these benefits and we grant them the honors they deserve.

But of course, a cool hour slips away, fits pass, difficulties mount, and most of us return to dodging the demands of this or that virtue and resenting the fact that we fall short of its measure. *This* resentment is an ordinary consequence of the difficulties that *every* virtue confronts, and notice, it does not deny the perfection resented. The imperfect resent the perfect because of the difficulties that divide them, and their resentment bears witness to the fact that they recognize the authority of that perfection and their failure to measure up. It is not, then, the kind of resentment that we find directed at tolerance, where the virtue is despised not as arduous excellence, but as vice in disguise. Both kinds of resentment follow from the difficulty and instability of virtue in general, but toleration's instability generates actions that encourage us to confuse the virtue and its semblances, the real thing and vices dressed in virtue's garb. This consequence of virtue's ordinary instability distinguishes tolerance from most other virtues, and this confusion causes a good portion of the resentment that attaches to the virtue itself. No doubt, semblances of virtue are frequently mistaken for the real thing, but as far as I can tell, this common confusion rarely follows from the difficulties and instabilities that afflict the virtues in general, and once it does emerge by other means with respect to other virtues, it does not, as far as I can tell, diminish our regard for them. Consider courage. As Aristotle points out, it has a number of semblances that we often mistake for true perfection, and yet rarely does this confusion come packaged with contempt for the virtue (*NE* 1116a17-1117a29). In fact, if anything, just the opposite is true. In our confusion we extend the admiration we have for courage to its semblances. But not so with tolerance, where confusion of true and apparent virtue typically generates suspicion of the virtue itself and resentment of the praise it so often receives. Moreover, these extraordinary inferences from an ordinary confusion seem easy to make, easy to imitate.

The argument goes like this. As a virtue, tolerance regards those objectionable activities and things that fall between two extremes, between the unbearably harmful and the harmlessly unobjectionable. The tolerant know which activities and things fall within this domain, and they respond to each as each deserves. Like all virtuous persons, they act with the constancy of habit, with ease and pleasure, with one eye on the good they hope to achieve and another on the good they find in the act of virtue itself. But of course, most of us fall short of perfect virtue. We act tolerantly in response to objectionable differences of little consequence but struggle with those that matter. When we succeed, it's only as we restrain ourselves — only as we choke down our outrage and stifle our desire to oppose the differences that we despise — and most of us find this act of self-restraint too difficult to muster much of the time. How can one despise and forbear at the same time anyway? So, more often than not, our imperfect tolerance, like our deficient courage, collapses into vicious moral postures. Confronted by difficulties that the tolerant address well — by judgments that are difficult to make and differences that are painful to endure — those of us with little virtue abandon our objection to what we at first, and quite rightly, found odious and instead cultivate some other attitude, perhaps indifference, perhaps acceptance. And notice, the vice cultivated is a semblance of the virtue, not the absence of its act. In most instances, the indifferent and the accepting act roughly as the tolerant do, but not from tolerant habits and motives. They dodge the virtue but not the act.

What follows is the now common confusion of tolerance with a couple of its semblances, of the real thing with some of its opposing vices dressed in virtue's clothing. Other virtues have semblances that enable the morally mediocre to pose among the virtuous from time to time, but few deteriorate under the demands of virtue's difficulty into a moral posture that can produce a semblance of virtue's act. Courage, for example, has semblances such as fearlessness that give the appearance of virtue in character and deed, and yet imperfect courage tends to collapse into fearful moral postures that are incapable of producing actions that resemble those caused by courage.[10] By contrast, imperfect tolerance tends to collapse under virtue's difficulty into moral postures that enable those without the virtue to act as the tolerant do, at least for the most part. As perfect tolerance is rare and painful differences are many, most assume that tolerance is nothing but these postures, nothing but blithe indifference that quickly melts into vile acceptance. Indeed, most of its critics are eager to assume that tolerance simply is this moral collapse. And of course, fearing moral collapse, some not only decry tolerance, but they flee to the *other* boundary of its domain. Looking for a solution to the problems of association that disagreement and difference invariably generate, unable to combine objection and endurance as the virtuous do, and appalled by the easy indifference and contemptible acceptance that are so often mistaken for tolerance, they reduce the harmlessly objectionable to the dangerously harmful and become advocates of law and order, of coercion and constraint.

10. See Aristotle, *NE* 1116b25-1117a4.

Such is our lot. Moral collapse or heavy-handed paternalism; these are the options that tolerance offers those of us who are morally mediocre (that's most of us!) and who cannot, as a result, resist the instability that comes packaged with virtue's difficulty. And yet many are convinced that these vices are not consequences of ordinary instability and weakness but are essential to tolerance itself. They are, after all, toleration's most common yield, or many assume so. Tolerance must then be a vice, just as the praise it receives nevertheless must be resented and its friends resisted.[11]

But of course, resentment that rests on a confusion, on the inability to distinguish true tolerance from its semblances, is hardly justified. What's needed, then, is a better account of the virtue, one that helps us escape this confusion. Three points deserve mention. First, every account of tolerance includes a discussion of its limits, of the indifferent and the acceptable on the one hand, and of the intolerable and potentially coercible on the other. To say that it does scarcely amounts to criticism. It is, rather, to say something mundane and true.

Second, because every account of tolerance comes loaded with concrete judgments about the tolerable and the intolerable, every account is open to dispute, not about tolerance itself, but about its substance, scope, and limits. This is inevitable.

Third, because tolerance is a virtue, the best way to resolve these disputes is to cultivate and acquire the habit of acting tolerantly. Why? Because we say people are tolerant when they are accepting, indifferent, enduring, and constraining with respect to the right actions and things, in the right circumstances, and to the right degree. Right judgment about concrete matters such as these is the very soul of this and every other moral virtue. But this means that tolerance itself cannot be justly resented simply because it includes these judgments, because they are difficult to make, or because the conflicts and disagreements that tolerance is supposed to address are frequently reproduced in our debates and contests over its substance, scope, and limits.

Of course, there will be winners and losers here, but the losers should lament their loss and the regime of tolerance that emerges, not that the matter was decided by contest and certainly not the virtue in dispute. Nor should tolerance be resented simply because those without the virtue in full measure are disposed to shun its difficult judgments and painful endurance by

11. For examples of this response, one from the right, one from the left, see Conyers 2001 and Brown 2008.

casting among the unbearably harmful those matters that ought to remain among the objectionable yet tolerable. What *can* be lamented is that societies like ours encourage this kind of vice, this corruption of tolerance. We tend to be relatively skittish about moral contest, and we tend to diffuse its sources by reducing matters that provoke disagreement to those that do not. There is nothing wrong with this strategy, not per se, but it does create the impression that moral judgment can be avoided (even when it can't be) and it does encourage us to resort to this strategy whenever judgment becomes difficult and disagreement likely. At times we should make this resort, at times we shouldn't. The tolerant will know how to distinguish these times, and yet because most of us fall short of perfect virtue, those who live in societies like ours will be encouraged by our surroundings to make this resort whenever and wherever difficulties and disagreements arise.

Such is the way we live now. At the same time, we should keep in mind that this dynamic reaches beyond tolerance to justice, its home and principle, and while we might, in some instances, bemoan the dynamic, few of us bewail *this* virtue. Those of us with ordinary measures of justice built into our souls surely dodge its difficulties more often than we should. We reduce judgments about the just and the unjust to calculations of utility. We sidestep rights and ignore wrongs. Still, no one regards justice with contempt simply because of its instability among the morally imperfect. Why then should we regard tolerance differently? If lament we must, then we should consider how few of us respond as the tolerant do to the differences that give us the most difficulty, that cause us the most pain. At the same time, we can't take this lament to a fever pitch without resenting the virtue itself. What we can decry is philosophers who encourage complaints and critics who provoke resentment simply because they overlook how tolerance stands among the other moral virtues and how the virtues in general stand among various difficulties.

Did Kuyper have thoughts like these when he considered the virtues in general and tolerance in particular? No, he didn't. As far as I can tell, he was not the sort of thinker who spent his days mapping the fine details of this or that virtue, whether tolerance or some other. At the same time, I don't think it can be denied that within his treatment of common grace we find the virtues praised for their ameliorative effects on the difficulties and dangers of human life. Common grace in its external operation keeps death and disorder at bay. It keeps creation in being and makes human flourishing possible, but it does not make human life easy, it does not guarantee that flourishing will come. It neither protects us from loss nor brings perfection to the various spheres of life. This is where the virtues come in, officers of the interior operations of common grace, and this is where Kuyper insists that the trials of this life are both the arena of their work and the background against which we measure their value. Pay attention to this background — as I have tried to do with respect to tolerance — and some of the puzzles that confound our understanding of the virtues come into focus. Some, perhaps, can even be resolved.[12]

References

Aquinas. 1948. *Summa Theologica.* Translated by Fathers of the English Dominican Province. Rev. ed. New York: Benzinger Brothers.

Aristotle. 2000. *Nicomachean Ethics.* Translated by T. H. Irwin. 2nd ed. Indianapolis: Hackett.

Augustine. 1998. *City of God against the Pagans.* Translated by R. W. Dyson. Cambridge: Cambridge University Press.

Bawer, B. 2005. "Tolerance or Death." *Reasononline,* November 30. http://www. reason.com/news/show/33002.html.

Brown, W. 2008. *Regulating Aversion: Tolerance in the Age of Identity and Empire.* Princeton: Princeton University Press.

Budziszewski, J. 1992. *True Tolerance: Liberalism and the Necessity of Judgment.* Piscataway, N.J.: Transaction.

Buruma, I. 2006. *Murder in Amsterdam: Liberal Europe, Islam, and the Limits of Tolerance.* New York: Penguin.

Conyers, A. J. 2001. *The Long March: How Toleration Made the World Safe for Power and Profit.* Dallas: Spence.

Fletcher, G. 1996. "The Instability of Tolerance." In *Toleration: An Elusive Virtue,* edited by D. Heyd, pp. 158-72. Princeton: Princeton University Press.

King, M. L., Jr. 1963. *Why We Can't Wait.* San Francisco: Harper and Row.

Kuyper, A. 1998a. "Common Grace." In *Abraham Kuyper: A Centennial Reader,* edited by J. Bratt, pp. 165-204. Grand Rapids: Eerdmans.

————. 1998b. "Common Grace in Science." In *Abraham Kuyper: A Centennial Reader,* edited by J. Bratt, pp. 441-60. Grand Rapids: Eerdmans.

12. I have focused on the relationship between the moral virtues and the difficulties they address under common grace, but I could just as well have attended to intellectual virtues. Thus Kuyper insists that before Adam was darkened by sin, he had immediate knowledge of the world. Not so for us: "to Adam, science was an immediate possession; for us it is bread we can eat only in the sweat of our minds, after hard and strenuous labor" (Kuyper 1998b: 451).

————. 1998c. "Sphere Sovereignty." In *Abraham Kuyper: A Centennial Reader,* edited by J. Bratt, pp. 461-90. Grand Rapids: Eerdmans.

Locke, J. 1983. *A Letter concerning Toleration.* Indianapolis: Hackett.

MacKinnon, K. 1989. *Toward a Feminist Theory of the State.* Cambridge: Harvard University Press.

Steyn, M. 2006. "It's the Demography, Stupid." *New Criterion* 24, no. 5, pp. 10-19.

Kuyper on Islam: A Summary and Translation

Rimmer de Vries

I

In 1905 Kuyper's Antirevolutionary Party lost the elections, and Kuyper ceased to be premier. Almost immediately he embarked on a carefully planned study tour around the Mediterranean. It lasted nine months, and he wrote up his findings and experiences in a large two-volume book titled *Om de Oude Wereldzee*. Wherever he went he encountered the powerful presence of Islam, which impressed him greatly and led him to comment on it in a number of articles and books. He wrote one special essay in volume 2 entitled "The Enigma of Islam." This related especially to his travels in the Middle East and North Africa, where the Christian church had once been strong and flourishing but now barely existed, except as ruins. How had this happened so rapidly? Whereas it took four centuries to establish the Christian church in the area, once Islam appeared like a meteor in Mecca, it was wiped out in less than a century, despite Christianity's being a "higher religion." What follows is a summary rather than a direct translation of the essay. But it follows Kuyper's own wording fairly closely while omitting some material of little contemporary interest.

II

In "The Enigma of Islam" Kuyper examines a number of explanations for the astonishing decline of Christianity in North Africa with the arrival of Islam. Although he attributes to Mohammed a strong visionary and ecstatic personality, he does not find any of the explanations wholly satisfactory. The first he discusses is the strict monotheism of the Islamic religion. It broke with all forms of polytheism (though even Mohammed, at one specially difficult time in his life, called on Allah, Ozza, and Murat, the latter two being false gods). Islam brought with it a new driving force and motivation. It was not a mixture of several other religions. The spiritual force behind Mohammed was his conviction that Allah was the only eternal God, the God of the Haniffiya who is merciful and should be revered. Monotheism is a powerful force and brought new motivation to the masses, though it required much courage to break with all forms of polytheism.

However, there was a further dimension. Mohammed's religion was not something confined to the inner room, outside the daily life of the believer, but affected all of life, penetrated all human existence and activity, society, government, etc. Allah's power embraced everything, and besides Allah nothing could be tolerated. The world was a powerful clock that Allah designed and controlled through a law and a will that determined everything — past, present, and future. Allah had always been, but people had not always understood the mystery of his reign. That is how Mohammed's revelation was connected with other revelations of monotheism. It was not a syncretism incorporating other religions, but part of a continuing process of revelation through many prophets such as Adam, Noah, Shem, Abraham, Moses, and Jesus, all of them advocates of monotheism. Jesus was the greatest before Mohammed. However, Allah's revelation did not end with Jesus. Jesus himself said that after him would come another Paraclete. With the revelation to Mohammed, the process was finished and complete. Thus the Muslim faith consisted of two tenets: the confession that Allah controlled everything, and that with Mohammed Allah's revelation was complete and closed.

The completeness of the revelation also meant that the faithful had to know about Allah's will, the laws and rules for all of life. Therein lay the importance of the Koran as well as the Hadith (the tradition) in the Sunnah, the *ijma* as the *vox populi* of the learned Muslims, and the *ijithad* (or doctrines reached by logical deduction). Nothing can be left for simple human approval. Everything has to be regulated by higher authority. Allah had to control his believers in all their breadth and depth. As a result there was a strong nomism that penetrated Islam as yeast. The battle for some freedom of the will applied only to moral responsibility. But the belief that all of life was controlled by Allah was central to Islam and gave it its unity and power. Devotion to Allah and observance of his will were one and the same.

This was the root of the Muslim's pride and the burden of conducting holy war, or jihad. Only the one who bows before Allah is a true human being and deserves his protection. Only Muslim believers should be in charge of government. If blood is spilled for minor causes, then certainly it is justified to do so in the honor of Allah. Because Islam was meant to be a world religion, and not a national one like Israel's, the case for holy war became even stronger. Mohammed's religion was absolute, a religion for the world, the only legitimate religion. It had no borders, so where there was resistance, war was justified. The jihad is therefore an indispensable element of the Islamic religion, rooted in its absolute monotheism and nomistic form. Kuyper makes reference to the ninth sura, verses 5 and 6: "The faithful must be prepared to wage war at all times. Kill then anyone who worships gods besides Allah, wherever you find them. Only if he accepts the required rules of the Islam religion may he be released." Even though the various schools later toned down this harsh commandment, the basic principle still stands. The Hanafits ruled that as long as somewhere a jihad was conducted, the rest of the believers were absolved from doing so, but the principle has never been abandoned. To thwart Allah is the greatest crime that can be committed and must be punished.

This strict nomistic monotheism has a democratic character and allows for some individual freedom because there is no authority between the believer and Allah — no priesthood — a principle that remained unaltered despite the later creation of a caliph, the sheik of Islam, and the *ulema* as powers. All believers were like the teeth of the same comb, Mohammed said. Islam rests on the confession of the believers. That is why there are so many divisions and sects among Muslims, even more than among Christians. But even so, they all feel themselves to be one body who call on Allah and the Prophet. The confession of Allah and the Prophet is key to everything. Believers may be slow in their prayers or giving or other demands made by the Koran and the Sunnah, but one thing is a must: they resist anyone who rejects Islam. Even though there may be differences over the caliphate or sherifate, a strong tie binds believers all over the world. That is why Mohammed did not make the caliphate hereditary or appoint a successor.

However, the dark side of Islam is its lack of spiritual depth. There is no second birth, no deep concern about sin, no soteriological content. Mohammed did give moral norms for marriage and the use of alcohol, and these went against the immoral customs of the Arabs at that time. But this was no more than a movement of the line. Mohammed himself violated the rule of having no more than four wives, while the concubines from among slave women lowered the moral character. There was not a rich family life among the Muslims, as the role and position of the women were low and divorce was easy. In the area of moral behavior there was always the system of accommodation. Since the final word was always that of Mohammed, it was difficult to move to a higher level of moral behavior. There was no conversion experience leading to better behavior, as in Christianity. From time to time there were attempts to develop more puritan moral behavior, especially under the Wahabites, but they never exceeded the rules and norms laid out in the Koran. There was never an ethical development stemming from basic moral principles. Christianity rests on three pillars: faith, hope, and love — or, put in organic terms, rebirth, faith, and sanctification. In Islam there are five pillars: faith in Allah and his prophet, the daily prayers, Ramadan fasting, charitable giving, and the pilgrimage to Mecca. This shows the external character that dominates the Muslim religion, while the expectation of paradise after this life reveals the same lack of moral standards. Although attempts were made to portray the paradise expectation in allegorical terms, the majority of Muslims understand it literally.

Some holier glow in this barren ethical system came from the side of mysticism in both its ascetic and its ecstatic forms. It was an essential element in a legalistic religion, but it remained mostly confined to small groups. In the Koran, which addressed the masses, there was rather little discussion of mysticism, though mysticism played a significant role in the dervish orders and in Sufism. Later it inspired pan-Islamism, which could not have taken off without the glow of mysticism. So even though one can argue that the Koran did not encourage strict asceticism, which came much later, long after Mohammed, it cannot be denied that Islam received some of its strength from mysticism. It is, after all, a Semitic religion with mystical elements that aim to achieve closer relations with God and thus assure a place in paradise. But as a rule, mysticism did not affect the application of ethical standards to society.

Had Islam remained a local religion for the Middle East, and Saudi Arabia in particular, its rapid development would have been understandable as it was a higher religion than prevailed in that region. The enigma is that it developed rapidly in a broader area where the Christian church was strong and had a yet higher form of religion and civilization than Islam. Its monotheistic character, the commandment to holy war and to win the world, and also the fighting spirit of the Arabs with their desire to plunder — all are factors to be taken into account. But they do not explain the rapid demise of the Christian church, especially in North Africa. By the seventh century there were strong churches everywhere and there were synods attended by five hundred or more bishops. There were important church leaders such as Origen, Athanasius, Cyprian, Augustine, and Tertullian who had studied in Egypt and Carthage. There had been severe persecutions, and martyrdom prevailed (for example, Perpetua). There were cathedrals and schools for the education of the clergy. The church was flourishing and had moved into the Sudan and Ethiopia. The Christian religion was not superficial but impacted people's daily lives. Yet, except for the Copts and a few Armenians, Marcionites, and Greeks, little is left of the glorious Byzantine Church. And all this happened at one strike, not over many ages. This can be explained only by the situation of the church at that time and the way Islam used its propaganda.

The Christian church at first grew through quiet evangelism and was thus very healthy. Soon, however, it was accepted in broader circles in which various forms of Greek and Asian philosophy prevailed, and made themselves masters of the mysteries of the gospel. Already in the second century the church had to battle with the Gnostics and the Docetists, and later with the Manicheans. In the East a feeling of dissatisfaction generated an inclination to incorporate each new form of religion in a syncretistic manner. The quiet growth of the humble Christian believers went on, certainly, but church leadership fell into the hands of a learned class who incorporated all kinds of non-Christian ideas. In this way, leaders drifted from the roots of Christianity, and more and more sought the essence of the faith in philosophical-dogmatic systems that did not look to holy inspiration but to barren scholastic dialectics. This placed pagan philosophical foundations under the edifice of the Christian religion. Bitter debates, centered mostly on the person of Christ, developed and divided the church. The mystery of the incarnation was no longer accepted in faith, but was rather explained by means of all kinds of philosophical reasoning. The church was compelled to intervene in these debates in a series of councils in order to neutralize the Arians, the Nestorians, the Monophysites, and the Monothylites. Sometimes the church used force. This tore the church apart, broke its unity, and at the same time weakened it by a loss of evangelistic zeal. Under Byzantium, the learned discussed the *dogma* of Christ; but the heart felt the *love* of Christ. The mystical union between Christ and the believer was steadily loosened.

In addition to philosophical dueling, dialectical divisions, and Byzantine coolness, a second force undermined real Christianity. That was caesaropapism. With the conversion of Constantine the Great, the church came under the power of the state. This created a great expansion of the church, since many people were compelled to join the church, even by force. Paganism was finished and the pagan temples were converted into churches. Yet the inner heart of the church weakened. People wore the Christian cloth, but inside they remained the same. In addition, church issues became state issues and the emperor became involved in church disputes. True, the great church councils remained independent, but once they had concluded it was the state that enforced their decisions. Thus the spiritual situation of the church deteriorated. It became a tool of politicians, intellectuals, and powerful church officials. Kuyper here draws attention to the letters to the seven churches in Revelation, where much of this was forewarned.

While in this miserable condition, the unexpected storm of Islam suddenly shook the church to its foundations. This only happened, of course, under the guidance of our Lord. Whoever believes that he is Lord over the church must see these happenings as a justifiable punishment of the faithlessness of the church. Not in the church of the East but in the church of the West would the Christian religion be victorious. So Kuyper laments the complete disappearance of the Christian church in North Africa and Asia. The Christian remnants in Turkey and Syria and elsewhere have actually incorporated some Islamic influences, but the same cannot be said of the Muslims. Islam is like the grasshopper plague that eats all the leaves off the tree and leaves the branches barren.

How did Islam bring this about? First, Muslims killed many pagans and Jews. Either accept Islam or face death. And many Jews who had abandoned their religion later helped the Muslims in their attack against the Christians. But how did Islam succeed against the Christians? Certainly they intimidated the Christians with their power and force, but how did they win over their hearts? The Muslims treated Christians differently from pagans and Jews because Christians also believed in Allah. At the same time, though they had the Old Testament and the New Testament, they did not have the Koran. Accordingly, they were tolerated as a lower class of sympathizers, and given some freedom of worship on condition that they acknowledge the higher authority of Islam.

This special status dominated relations between Muslims and all other people throughout the area. Since Allah was all in all, the Muslims deserved to have the leadership positions in the world. Only they actually had the right to exist. The head of Islam was Allah's representative. In 629 (or 627, according to some), seven years after the Hijra (or five), Mohammed sent letters to the rulers of the countries, including the king of Persia and the emperor in Constantinople, requesting them to convert to Islam and bring their countries and peoples under the prophet in Mecca. These letters, sealed with the notation from "Mohammed, the ambassador of Allah," impressed the rulers. Those in Saudi Arabia agreed. Those in Ethiopia gave a friendly response. The Byzantine viceroy in Egypt sent Mohammed two Coptic women for his harem. Emperor Heraclites answered in gracious terms. Only Chosroes II, king of Persia, tore up the letter in a fury and ordered his general to find and arrest Mohammed.

From this episode, the position Mohammed took against all authorities from the very beginning is clear, even though he controlled only a very small part of Arabia. He had a firm understanding of the commandments of Allah for the entire world. Islam negotiated with everyone from a superior position and demanded capitulation. That meant that all rulers had to accept the authority of Islam, and any peace agreement was a privilege. Non-Muslims lived by the grace of Muslims. One had the choice: either accept Islam and be included among the believers, or pay a head tax called *jizya* and then became a *dhimmi* or die by the sword. However, even the payment of the head tax was an act of submission. The purpose was to suppress and humiliate the Christians socially.

For example, when Omar captured Jerusalem he set the terms of capitulation: the Christians could worship freely in their churches and chapels but on condition that every Muslim at all times, day and night, could be present; that the worship service could never be on the street in the open; that Christian children could not look in the Koran; that Christians could not convert Muslims or prevent others from becoming Muslims; that in meetings the best seats must be given to Muslims; that Christians could not be dressed as Muslims; that Christians could not write in Arabic; that they could not adopt Muslim names; that they could not ride on a large saddle; that they could not carry arms; that they must shave off their beards; that no crosses be placed on buildings; that they could not ring church bells; that they must bury their dead without any ceremony; that they could not have Muslim slaves; that they could not look in houses of Muslims; that they would not raise their hands against Muslims. These terms of capitulation applied to parents and children, and noncompliance with them could mean death. In Egypt there were additional terms such as the requirement to wear large wooden crosses of several pounds around the neck and to wear very dark unsightly garments. All this served to impress upon Christians that Muslims were a superior sort of human being and that in public only Muslims were complete persons.

So the Christians were excluded from social life. Soon the head tax became an important source of funds for the caliph, and he did not like it when this flow of funds dried up as Christians converted to Islam. These head taxes paid for the building of the great mosque in Jerusalem. All these social humiliations contributed to the conversion of Christians.

In the first phase, Islam developed a very high level of intellectual life. For four centuries the Arabs were the masters of scientific endeavor. Islam claimed all life, religious and social, political, juridical, etc. There was a growing desire to bring all this knowledge into an Islamic system and order. The principles of the Koran had to be applied to all areas of inquiry. Many schools emerged that developed various interpretations. They used Greek philosophy and attracted the leading scholars of the time, while the Christians who had lost their schools were increasingly isolated and marginalized. Islam always had a school attached to the mosque. Because the system depended on memorization and inculcated received opinion rather than developing creative thinking, all criticism was excluded. When a Muslim encountered a non-Muslim, he knew exactly what to say. Finally, Muslims accused Christians of serving two Gods. The Muslims revered Jesus over Moses and held a purer understanding of him, without all the dogmatic details. This was a successful form of propaganda.

Kuyper discusses at length the Al-Azhar University in Cairo. It was the largest educational institution of its day, and after a period of decline became the center of spiritual and scientific research in Islam. Established in 975 by Kaid Djawhar of the Fatimids, at one time it had 20,000 students. The Fatimidic caliphs were originally Shia followers of Ali and opposed the caliph in Baghdad. The Baghdad schools considered the Fatimids heretics, hence the need to establish their own schools. This was the origin of the great Cairo University. It attracted the best scholars among the Arabs by paying large salaries and bestowing honors. During two centuries of debates between Baghdad and Cairo, the latter normally had the last word. Salah-al-Din, or Saladin, ended this discussion when he captured Egypt. He restored the authority of the Baghdad caliphs and joined the Sunnis, but he did not want to alienate the Egyptian scholars. So he ruled that the Shafites could stay but on the condition that three other Muslim schools of Sunnis would be represented in the university's faculty (Hannifites, Malakites, and Hanbalites). Everyone had full freedom to teach his branch of theology and jurisprudence. As a result, the reputation of Al-Azhar rose even more, and it became the center of learning for all Muslims in theology, law, literary sciences, science, natural science, mathematics, and astrology. Later, the Turkish occupation set this period of growth back, as the Turks had other values.

But there was also this factor. The development of Islamic learning had peaked. Its scholasticism was complete and stifled the development of Islamic knowledge, thus leading to a highly conservative character that continues to this day. Even so, this same conservative character contributed to the staying power of Islam.

Kuyper continues by describing in some detail his personal experience at the Al-Azhar University. Teaching is done mostly in the open air or in courtyards, since the weather is almost always beautifully sunny. Students are free to join, listen, and interrupt to ask questions. As a rule the rector is of the Shafite school and follows the Fatimid tradition. An entrance exam is not necessary. Anyone can take part, including children and small girls. They begin with reading, writing, and Arabic grammar. Thereafter they learn simple verses from the Koran. Eventually they learn commentaries, rhetoric, poetry, etc. The entire school period can last fifteen to sixteen years if a child begins at the age of six. There is no final exam. At the end, the student receives the title "Sheik."

One can eat simple food in school while water is being carried by special water carriers all day. Uniforms are available for the needy. There are dormitories where some forty students live together in one large room, but each has a niche in the wall for study. There are guards everywhere to keep order. Mischief in the classroom is punished quickly. Students can earn some money by providing services. They have three months of vacation, which they use to return home to earn some additional money and to propagate Islam. In fact, this is something they do all their lives without pay. The senior professors advise the government.

Kuyper concludes this section by pointing out once more that Islam strives to be a world power. Jesus, on the other hand, always stressed that God's kingdom was not of this world. For the Muslim, this world is *his* world and that gives him much self-esteem and the sense that he is an aristocrat in this world. This sense was attractive to divided Christians. Moreover, since the Byzantine state church frequently treated Christian sects harshly, at times the Muslims were welcomed as saviors. Just as Protestants in France welcomed the French Revolution in 1789 because it freed them from the oppression of the Roman Catholic Church, so persecuted Christian sects welcomed the Arabs as liberators. Also, it was not uncommon that when rulers changed, the form of religion changed. Since Islam also acknowledged Jesus, it was fairly easy to convert exhausted Christians to Islam. Its rules and forms were simple to follow, and thus provided welcome relief from the complicated debates of Christian teachers. Yet, even in the light of all these considerations,

Kuyper remains mystified about how the higher Christian religion could disappear so quickly under the power and propaganda of Islam.

Kuyper now discusses the situation of Islam in the world of his day, where it was showing considerable toughness despite a decline. Intellectual and scientific life was stultified, partly because its ideas were fixed and frozen. Having declared their system of orthodoxy "complete," the Sunnis, and particularly the Hanafits, engaged mostly in defense of the tradition rather than the development of further thought. There were attempts by "young Turks" and "young Egyptians" to separate religion from the state and introduce Western-style governments, but these attempts failed. The broad masses stuck to the tradition, and it did not take much to inflame them to renewed fanaticism. The influence of Islam as a world power had weakened because of internal disagreements. The Turks for a while restored the unity of Islam and brought much under the Turkish reign. But after the battle of Lepanto in 1571 this unity of power again began to break down. The battle of Trafalgar left the British masters of the Mediterranean. Moreover, since the Muslims were better warriors than administrators, the real positions of influence in governments in matters of finance, diplomacy, and administration fell into the hands of Copts, Armenians, and Greeks. Yet, despite all this, the Muslim religion had maintained itself among the masses. Around 1900 the Muslims totaled about 245 million people, or 15 percent of the world's population. Of this total, 145 million were in Asia, 50 million in Africa, 12 million in Europe, and 30 million in Indonesia.

Kuyper discusses in some detail the various countries where there are Muslims. Persia is the most independent country with a mixture of Sunnis and Shias. It also maintains a monarchy and rejected the caliphs. Their allegiance is to Ali, whom they consider the incarnation of the Godhead. The Afghanis also have both Sunnis and Shias. Islam in India has grown at the expense of the Hindus. Their caste system suppresses the poor, who accordingly looked on Islam as liberating. The Muslims in India recognize the sultan of Turkey as spiritual head; they are orthodox and stand above the Hindus in cultural matters. The British government more and more listens to the Muslims. The history of the Muslim population in China is interesting. A group of Arabs helped the ruling dynasty to stay in power, and ever since, the Chinese emperors have treated the Muslims with kindness and given them positions of power. So even though the Muslims constituted only one-twentieth of the Chinese population, they were always a force to be reckoned with.

Turkey remains the main Islamic power, partly because of the caliphate of the sultan, partly because it is an independent power, and partly because of its powerful army. It constitutes the historical continuation of the original Islamic world power. In all mosques around the world prayers are offered for the sultan of Turkey. The building of the railway system from Damascus to Medina will help the Turks to keep Arabia and the surrounding areas under control.

Thus Islam was spiritually strong. As a political power, though, it was weak, with only one-fourth of its believers (18 million) living under an independent-power Muslim government — Turkey. Muslims rule over non-Muslims as their calling and privilege, but they are not allowed to be subjected to other authorities. When this does happen, a condition is created in which a Muslim may have to subdue himself fatalistically, though his soul continues in resistance and looks forward to the time of redemption and renewal that will be brought by the restoration of his own Muslim government. The Turkish military, however, was incapable of such a restoration.

Out of this feeling of hopelessness and helplessness, with its combination of internal religious resilience and external lack of power, was born pan-Islamism. Islam was politically dispersed but spiritually still united, as the Shias were small in numbers. Even the arguments among the four schools had ended with the victory of the Hanafits. So there was still a fixed form of worship, but it was in need of revival. At first the *muftis* and the *ulemas* objected to this movement, since they wanted to maintain the public worship in the mosque above the drive to deeper religious experience. They did not want to see the rise of monasteries over mosques. Kuyper mentions a similar reaction in Holland after the French period, when the official established church forcefully resisted the emergence of conventicles and similar groups. But eventually the sultan gave in and extended his blessing to the reform movement, which might otherwise have appointed the sheriff of Mecca as the pope of Islam.

Pan-Islamism was a religious movement, not a national movement. It aimed to do three things: (1) strengthen the unity under the sign of the half moon; (2) remove or purify all foreign elements from the Muslim religion; and (3) revive the petrified faith. The sheiks sent missionaries to Africa and Asia to revive the faith of the people. While the threat of European power was a strong inducement and motivation to bring about this revival, politically the ultimate goal was to bring all Muslims again under the caliph. The main objective was the purification of the faith and preparation of the faithful for martyrdom. The movement proved to be very successful, and the colonial powers became much more careful not to offend the Muslims in countries like the Sudan and Egypt.

However, military superiority does not translate into spiritual power. Nor does it break spiritual resistance so much as strengthen it. Even the hope and expectation that the higher culture of Western civilization would subdue the Muslim culture proved false. Muslims know how to benefit from Western technology and governmental structures, while the heart of the faithful remains untouched. The slogan for Mohammed and against Jesus Christ remains. Kuyper mentions the story of a modern Muslim woman who expressed her feeling of wishing to behead every Christian missionary. Another important gentleman said he had to control the urge to kill every time he passed by an English sentry. As a result, we can help develop economically Muslim countries, but they will bless the day when we leave them alone.

There is only one way to capture the hearts and loyalty of the people, and that is for them to adopt the Christian faith, but there is little prospect of this. Christian missions have been active in the sultan lands but always meet great resistance. First the French, then the Italians and Greeks, and more recently English and American missions have worked very hard and with much perseverance in Asiatic Turkey, but the fruits are small and mainly a revival of the remnants of earlier Christian groups. Missions were able to attract people to their schools and hospitals, but did not reach their hearts. The same is true of the Dutch in Indonesia. One would deceive oneself to expect the conversion of Muslims in large numbers. For the Muslim, conversion to Christianity is descending to a lower level of religion. Islam superseded Christianity and Islam has a higher level of revelation. To convert to Christianity would be an act of treason, and the entire community would pressure the convert to change his mind. Moreover, Christian missionaries bring with them Western forms with which Easterners do not feel comfortable.

The Christian missions plow on rocks, while Islam still makes plenty of progress in Africa and India. The Islamic faith is simple to understand, adoptable, charming, and attractive. Nevertheless, although the minarets daily call Allah the merciful God and ask for his mercies, a deep understanding and realization of sin and a desire for reconciliation with God are absent. Allah remains a mighty ruler who treats his servants favorably. Islam does not know a Father in the heavens who appeals to his children with the prayer "Be reconciled to God." Allah is identified with power, but lacks the holiness that is realized through redemption. The ideal of Holy Love is lacking in Islam and even in Allah.

In conclusion, Islam stands in the way of reaching a higher level of culture. It is no doubt a much higher culture than paganism, and from the seventh through thirteenth centuries it developed to very high levels. But it has settled down to a middling form of culture. Islam is a religion for men, and women are outside. In France you see churches filled with women only; in Islam women have hardly any role in the worship service. The great contributions women can bring to the social life of the nation and in the development of the culture to higher levels are excluded under Islam. Kuyper cites some women authors who have studied the treatment of women, including in the harems. They concluded that in many cases men behave like animals, and at totally unacceptable levels. The lack of female participation deprives Islam of the tenderness and warmth that women bring to the Christian religion.

On the other hand, Muslims are hospitable to strangers and benevolent to the poor. Kuyper cites a recent book, *Contrasts of Social Progress,* by Tenney, who points out that the level of philanthropy in London exceeded by ten times the generosity of Muslims in Constantinople. Muslims are honest in trade and commerce and compare favorably with the business behavior of Greeks, Armenians, and Asiatic Jews. Muslims are allowed to make small ethical mistakes as the fourth sura covers all small sins.

So while its political power has been broken, the spiritual condition of Islam remains healthy and has even gained vitality. The call for holy war that could bring about a bloodbath will not be able to reestablish its position as a political world power, but nevertheless its desire for world dominance remains. The half moon of Islam is far from its decline and not a negligible quantity. The Christians under the caliphs became Muslims, but Muslims living in Christian countries remained faithful to the Prophet Mohammed.

December 24, 1907